Vanderaook

Reach the Highest Standard in Professional Learning: Learning Designs

Volumes in the Reach the Highest Standard in Professional Learning Series

Learning Communities

Leadership

Resources

Data

Learning Designs

Implementation

Outcomes

Reach the Highest Standard in Professional Learning: Learning Designs

Eleanor Drago-Severson
Patricia Roy
Valerie von Frank

A Joint Publication

FOR INFORMATION:

Corwin

A SAGE Company

2455 Teller Road

Thousand Oaks, California 91320

(800) 233-9936

www.corwin.com

SAGE Publications Ltd.

1 Oliver's Yard

55 City Road

London EC1Y 1SP

United Kingdom

SAGE Publications India Pvt. Ltd.

B 1/I 1 Mohan Cooperative Industrial Area

Mathura Road, New Delhi 110 044

India

SAGE Publications Asia-Pacific Pte. Ltd.

3 Church Street

#10-04 Samsung Hub

Singapore 049483

Copyright © 2015 by Corwin and Learning Forward

All rights reserved. When forms and sample documents are included, their use is authorized only by educators, local school sites, and/or noncommercial or nonprofit entities that have purchased the book. Except for that usage, no part of this book may be reproduced or utilized in any form or by any means, electronic or mechanical, including photocopying, recording, or by any information storage and retrieval system, without permission in writing from the publisher.

All trade names and trademarks recited, referenced, or reflected herein are the property of their respective owners who retain all rights thereto.

Printed in the United States of America.

A catalog record of this book is available from the Library of Congress.

ISBN 978-1-4522-9201-4

This book is printed on acid-free paper.

Acquisitions Editor: Dan Alpert

Associate Editor: Kimberly Greenberg

Editorial Assistant: Cesar Reyes

Production Editor: Cassandra Margaret Seibel

Copy Editor: Kate Macomber Stern

Typesetter: C&M Digitals (P) Ltd.

Proofreader: Alison Syring

Indexer: Terri Corry

Cover Designer: Gail Buschman

Marketing Manager: Stephanie Trkay

SFI label applies to text stock

14 15 16 17 18 10 9 8 7 6 5 4 3 2 1

Contents

Introduction to the Series

These are the demands on educators and school systems right now, among many others:

- They must fulfill the moral imperative of educating every child for tomorrow's world, regardless of background or status.
- They must be prepared to implement college- and career-ready standards and related assessments.
- They must implement educator evaluations tied to accountability systems.

A critical element in creating school systems that can meet these demands is building the capacity of the system's educators at all levels, from the classroom teacher to the instructional coach to the school principal to the central office administrator, and including those partners who work within and beyond districts. Building educator capacity in this context requires effective professional learning.

Learning Forward's Standards for Professional Learning define the essential elements of and conditions for professional learning that leads to changed educator practices and improved student results. They are grounded in the understanding that the ultimate purpose of professional learning is increasing student success. Educator effectiveness—and this includes all educators working in and with school systems, not just teachers—is linked closely to student learning. Therefore increasing the effectiveness of educators is a key lever to school improvement.

Effective professional learning happens in a culture of continuous improvement, informed by data about student and educator performance and supported by leadership and sufficient resources.

Educators learning daily have access to information about relevant instructional strategies and resources and, just as important, time for collaboration with colleagues, coaches, and school leaders. Education leaders and systems that value effective professional learning provide not only sufficient time and money but also create structures that reinforce monitoring and evaluation of that learning so they understand what is effective and have information to adjust and improve.

WHY STANDARDS?

Given that any system can—and must—develop expertise about professional learning, why are standards important? Among many reasons are these:

First, adherence to standards ensures equity. When learning leaders across schools and systems agree to follow a common set of guidelines, they are committing to equal opportunities for all the learners in those systems. If all learning is in alignment with the Standards for Professional Learning and tied to student and school improvement goals, then all educators have access to the best expertise available to improve their practice and monitor results.

Standards also provide a common language that allows for conversation, collaboration, and implementation planning that crosses state, regional, and national borders. This collaboration can leverage expertise from any corner of the world to change practice and results.

Finally, standards offer guidelines for accountability. While an endorsement of the standards doesn't in itself guarantee quality, they provide a framework within which systems can establish measures to monitor progress, alignment, and results.

FROM STANDARDS TO TRANSFORMATION

So a commitment to standards is a first critical step. Moving into deep understanding and sustained implementation of standards is another matter. Transforming practices, and indeed, whole systems, will require long-term study, planning, and evaluation.

Reach the Highest Standard in Professional Learning is created to be an essential set of tools to help school and system leaders take those steps. As with the Standards for Professional Learning themselves, there will be seven volumes, one for each standard.

While the standards were created to work in synergy, we know that educators approach professional learning from a wide range of experiences, concerns, expertise, and passions. Perhaps a school leader may have started PLCs in his school to address a particular learning challenge, and thus has an abiding interest in how learning communities can foster teacher quality and better results. Maybe a central office administrator started her journey to standards-based professional learning through a study of how data informs changes, and she wants to learn more about the foundations of data use. This series was created to support such educators and to help them continue on their journey of understanding systemwide improvement and the pieces that make such transformation possible.

In developing this series of books on the Standards for Professional Learning, Corwin and Learning Forward envisioned that practitioners would enter this world of information through one particular book, and that their needs and interests would take them to all seven as the books are developed. The intention is to serve the range of needs practitioners bring and to support a full understanding of the elements critical to effective professional learning.

All seven volumes in Reach the Highest Standard in Professional Learning share a common structure, with components to support knowledge development, exploration of changes in practice, and a vision of each concept at work in real-world settings.

In each volume, readers will find

- A think piece developed by a leading voice in the professional learning field. These thought leaders represent both scholars and practitioners, and their work invites readers to consider the foundations of each standard and to push understanding of those seven standards.
- An implementation piece that helps readers put the think piece and related ideas into practice, with tools for both individuals and groups to use in reflection and discussion about the standards. Shirley M. Hord and Patricia Roy, longstanding Learning Forward standards leaders, created the implementation pieces across the entire series.
- A case study that illuminates what it looks like in schools and districts when education leaders prioritize the standards in

their improvement priorities. Valerie von Frank, with many years of writing about education in general and professional learning in particular, reported these pieces, highlighting insights specific to each standard.

MOVING TOWARD TRANSFORMATION

We know this about effective professional learning: Building awareness isn't enough to change practice. It's a critical first piece, and these volumes will help in knowledge development. But sustaining knowledge and implementing change require more.

Our intention is that the content and structure of the volumes can move readers from awareness to changes in practice to transformation of systems. And of course transformation requires much more. Commitment to a vision for change is an exciting place to start. A long-term informed investment of time, energy, and resources is non-negotiable, as is leadership that transcends one visionary leader who will inevitably move on.

Ultimately, it will be the development of a culture of collective responsibility for all students that sustains improvement. We invite you to begin your journey toward developing that culture through study of the Standards for Professional Learning and through Reach the Highest Standard in Professional Learning. Learning Forward will continue to support the development of knowledge, tools, and evidence that inform practitioners and the field. Next year's challenges may be new ones, and educators working at their full potential will always be at the core of reaching our goals for students.

Stephanie Hirsh
Executive Director, Learning Forward

The Learning Forward Standards for Professional Learning

Learning Communities: Professional learning that increases educator effectiveness and results for all students occurs within learning communities committed to continuous improvement, collective responsibility, and goal alignment.

Leadership: Professional learning that increases educator effectiveness and results for all students requires skillful leaders who develop capacity, advocate, and create support systems for professional learning.

Resources: Professional learning that increases educator effectiveness and results for all students requires prioritizing, monitoring, and coordinating resources for educator learning.

Data: Professional learning that increases educator effectiveness and results for all students uses a variety of sources and types of student, educator, and system data to plan, assess, and evaluate professional learning.

Learning Designs: Professional learning that increases educator effectiveness and results for all students integrates theories, research, and models of human learning to achieve its intended outcomes.

Implementation: Professional learning that increases educator effectiveness and results for all students applies research on change and sustains support for implementation of professional learning for long-term change.

Outcomes: Professional learning that increases educator effectiveness and results for all students aligns its outcomes with educator performance and student curriculum standards.

Source: Learning Forward. (2011). *Standards for Professional Learning.* Oxford, OH: Author.

The Learning Designs Standard

Professional learning that increases educator effective-
ness and results for all students integrates theories,
research, and models of human learning to achieve its
intended outcomes.

Integrating theories, research, and models of human learning into the planning and design of professional learning contributes to its effectiveness. Several factors influence decisions about learning designs, including the goals of the learning, characteristics of the learners, their comfort with the learning process and one another, their familiarity with the content, the magnitude of the expected change, educators' work environment, and resources available to support learning. The design of professional learning affects its quality and effectiveness.

APPLY LEARNING THEORIES, RESEARCH, AND MODELS

Cognitive psychologists, neuroscientists, and educators have studied how learning occurs for nearly a century. The resulting theories, research, and models of human learning shape the underlying framework and assumptions educators use to plan and design professional learning. While multiple designs exist, many have common features, such as active engagement, modeling, reflection, metacognition, application, feedback, ongoing support, and formative and summative assessment, that support change in knowledge, skills, dispositions, and practice.

Professional learning occurs in face-to-face, online, and hybrid settings. Some professional learning focuses on individual learning, while other forms focus on team-based or whole-school learning. Most professional learning occurs as a part of the workday, while other forms occur outside the school day. Both formal and informal designs facilitate and organize educator learning. Some learning designs use structured processes such as courses or workshops. Others are more fluid to allow for adjustments in the learning process. Some learning designs require team members or external experts as facilitators, while others are individually organized. Learning designs use synchronous or asynchronous interactions, live or simulated models and experiences, and print and nonprint resources to present information, model skills and procedures, provide low-risk practice, and support transfer to the workplace.

Job-embedded learning designs engage individuals, pairs, or teams of educators in professional learning during the workday. Designs for job-embedded learning include analyzing student data, case studies, peer observation or visitations, simulations, co-teaching with peers or specialists, action research, peer and expert coaching, observing and analyzing demonstrations of practice, problem-based learning, inquiry into practice, student observation, study groups, data analysis, constructing and scoring assessments, examining student or educator work, lesson study, video clubs, professional reading, or book studies. Learners and facilitators of learning may weave together multiple designs within on-site, online, or hybrid learning to achieve identified goals and to differentiate learning designs to meet the unique needs of individual learners. Learning designs that occur during the workday and engage peers in learning facilitate ongoing communication about learning, develop a collaborative culture with peer accountability, foster professionalism, and support transfer of the learning to practice.

Technology is rapidly enhancing and extending opportunities for professional learning. It particularly facilitates access to, sharing, construction, and analysis of information to enhance practice. Technology exponentially increases possibilities for personalizing, differentiating, and deepening learning, especially for educators who have limited access to on-site professional learning or who are eager to reach beyond the boundaries of their own work setting to join local or global networks to enrich their learning.

SELECT LEARNING DESIGNS

When choosing designs for professional learning, educators consider multiple factors. The first is the intended outcome, drawn from analysis of student and educator learning needs. Learning designs that engage adult learners in applying the processes they are expected to use facilitate the learning of those behaviors by making them more explicit. Effective designs for professional learning assist educators in moving beyond comprehension of the surface features of a new idea or practice to developing a more complete understanding of its purposes, critical attributes, meaning, and connection to other approaches. To increase student learning, educator learning provides many opportunities for educators to practice new learning with ongoing assessment, feedback, and coaching so the learning becomes fully integrated into routine behaviors.

Educators are responsible for taking an active role in selecting and constructing learning designs that facilitate their own and others' learning. They choose appropriate learning designs to achieve their individual, team, or school goals. Educators' learning characteristics and preferences also inform decisions about learning designs. Learners' backgrounds, experiences, beliefs, motivation, interests, cognitive processes, professional identity, and commitment to school and school system goals affect how educators approach professional learning and the effectiveness of various learning designs. Decisions about learning designs consider all phases of the learning process, from knowledge and skill acquisition to application, reflection, refinement, assessment, and evaluation. Learning designers consider how to build knowledge, develop skills, transform practice, challenge attitudes and beliefs, and inspire action.

PROMOTE ACTIVE ENGAGEMENT

Active engagement in professional learning promotes change in educator practice and student learning. Active engagement occurs when learners interact during the learning process with the content and with one another. Educator collaborative learning consistently produces strong, positive effects on achievement of learning outcomes. Active engagement respects adults as professionals and gives them significant voice and choice in shaping their own learning. Through active engagement, educators construct personal meaning of their learning, are more committed to its success, and identify authentic applications for their learning. Active learning processes promote deep understanding of new learning and increase motivation to implement it. Active learning processes include discussion and dialogue, writing, demonstrations, inquiry, reflection, metacognition, co-construction of knowledge, practice with feedback, coaching, modeling, and problem solving. Through exploration of individual and collective experiences, learners actively construct, analyze, evaluate, and synthesize knowledge and practices.

Source: Learning Forward. (2011). *Standards for Professional Learning.* Oxford, OH: Author.

About the Authors

Eleanor (Ellie) Drago-Severson is a Professor of Education Leadership and Adult Learning & Leadership at Teachers College, Columbia University. As a developmental psychologist, her work is inspired by the idea that schools must be places where adults and children can grow. She is dedicated to creating the conditions to achieve this and to helping school leaders and educators of all kinds to do the same on behalf of supporting adults and youth. Ellie's work builds bridges between research and practice by supporting teachers, principals, assistant principals, super-intendents, and other school and district leaders in their professional and personal development and growth. Ellie is author of five recent books: *Becoming Adult Learners: Principles and Practices for Effective Development* (Teachers College Press, 2004), *Helping Teachers Learn: Principal Leadership for Adult Growth and Development* (Corwin, 2004), *Leading Adult Learning: Supporting Adult Development in our Schools* (Corwin and Learning Forward, 2009), *Helping Educators Grow: Practices and Strategies for Supporting Leadership Development* (Harvard Education Press, 2012), and *Learning for Leadership: Developmental Strategies for Building Capacity in Our Schools* (Corwin, 2013). Learning Forward (formerly the National Staff Development Council, NSDC) awarded the Outstanding Staff Development Book of the Year in 2004 to *Helping Teachers Learn,* and selected *Leading Adult Learning* as their book of the month in the Fall 2009. Ellie is currently completing *The Art of Feedback: Tell Me So I Can Hear You* (Harvard Education Press, forthcoming). Ellie teaches, conducts research, and consults with education leaders and organizations on professional and personal growth and learning, leadership that supports principal, faculty and school development, capacity building, leadership development, coaching, qualitative research, and mentoring K–12 schools, university contexts, and ABE/ESOL (Adult Basic Education/English for Speakers of Other Languages) contexts. She is also an internationally certified developmental coach (i.e., Immunity to Change coaching), who works with principals, assistant principals, district leaders, and teachers to build internal individual and school capacity to achieve goals. She served as lead researcher on the Adult Development Team of the National Center for the Study of Adult Learning and Literacy (NCSALL) at Harvard University and as teacher, program designer, program director, and currently as consultant and professional developer in a variety of educational contexts, including K–12 schools and districts, higher education, adult education centers, and ABE/ESOL programs (domestically and internationally). Her work explores the promise of practices that support adult development, leadership development, and capacity building, within schools and districts, as well as across school systems. Ellie's work has been recognized by and supported with awards from the Spencer Foundation, the Klingenstein Foundation, and Harvard Graduate School of Education (HGSE), where she served as Lecturer in Education for eight years. While serving at Harvard, Ellie was awarded the 2005 Morningstar Award for Excellence in Teaching. Most recently, she received three outstanding teaching awards from Teachers College. She has earned degrees from Long Island University (BA) and Harvard University (EdM, EdD, and a post-doctoral fellowship). Ellie grew up in the Bronx, New York, and lives in New York City.

 **Dr. Patricia Roy** is a senior consultant with Learning Forward's Center for Results. She works with state departments of education, districts, and schools across the United States as well as internationally. Most recently, she developed briefings and a resource guide to help schools use results from the revised Standards Assessment Inventory (SAI2) to improve professional learning. She has authored many articles and chapters on effective professional development, school improvement, innovation configuration maps, and cooperative learning. In her work with Learning Forward, Pat developed professional

learning resource toolkits for Georgia; Arkansas; and Rochester, New York. She co-authored, with Joellen Killion, *Becoming a Learning School* and with Stephanie Hirsh, Joellen Killion, and Shirley Hord, *Standards Into Practice: Innovation Configurations for School-Based Roles* (2012). For 5 years, she wrote columns about implementing the Standards for Professional Development for *The Learning Principal* and *The Learning System,* two Learning Forward newsletters. She has also served as faculty for Professional Development Leadership Academy through the Arizona Department of Education. This 3-year program developed the knowledge and skills of school and district teams to plan, implement, and evaluate professional learning. She has also served as the founding director of the Delaware Professional Development Center in Dover, Deleware. The Center, developed by the Delaware State Education Association, focused on school improvement for student achievement and effective professional learning. She also served as the director of the Center for School Change in connection with a National Science Foundation SSI grant, a district coordinator of staff development, and an administrator in a regional educational consortium in Minnesota. Creating and improving professional learning so that it impacts student achievement is one of Pat's passions.

Valerie von Frank is an author, editor, and communications consultant. A former newspaper editor and education reporter, she has focused much of her writing on education issues, including professional learning. She served as communications director in an urban school district and a nonprofit school reform organization and was the editor of *JSD,* the flagship magazine for the National Staff Development Council, now Learning Forward, for 7 years. She has written extensively for education publications, including *JSD, Tools for Schools, The Learning System, The Learning Principal,* and *T3.* She is coauthor with Ann Delehant of *Making Meetings Work: How to Get Started, Get Going, and Get It Done* (Corwin, 2007), with Linda Munger of *Change, Lead, Succeed* (National Staff Development Council, 2010), with Robert Garmston of *Unlocking Group Potential to Improve Schools* (Corwin, 2012), and with Jennifer Abrams of *The Multigenerational Workplace: Communicate, Collaborate, and Create Community* (Corwin, 2014).

CHAPTER ONE

Helping Adults Learn

The Promise of Designing Spaces for Development

Eleanor Drago-Severson

> *Professional learning that increases educator effectiveness and results for all students* **integrates theories, research, and models of human learning to achieve its intended outcomes.** [Emphasis in original]
>
> Learning Forward, the Learning
> Designs Standard, 2011, p. 40

W hy should we focus on creating conditions that effectively support adult learning? Why is it essential to have a Learning Designs standard to guide our professional learning in schools and districts?

Put simply, the challenges of teaching and leading schools and school systems today are arguably more complex than ever before, regardless of our roles. Educators throughout our school systems—principals, assistant principals, teachers, school- and district-level leaders, professional developers, coaches, and policy makers—face unprecedented demands that are arguably *adaptive* in nature (Heifetz, 1994; Kegan & Lahey, 2001, 2009). These murkier kinds of challenges are difficult to identify, and must be addressed and resolved "in the act" of working on them (Wagneret al., 2006, p. 10). They require something different from us, something more. Unlike technical challenges (e.g., developing a school website, learning advanced technological skills), which can be addressed by increasing our knowledge, skills and expertise, or by hiring an expert to help solve them, the mounting adaptive challenges that we face in education—such as implementing Common Core State Standards for college and career readiness, caring for students' diverse needs, closing the achievement gap, working effectively in an era of high-stakes accountability, and navigating new teacher and principal evaluation systems—require teachers and school leaders to continuously learn and grow as they manage these tremendously complex issues and programs and ambiguity inherent in them. All of these challenges—both technical and adaptive—are demanding and make designing effective professional learning opportunities of paramount importance. The call for creating the conditions for authentic and deep professional learning experiences in our schools and systems is urgent (Drago-Severson, Maslin-Ostrowski, & Hoffman, 2013).

Learning Forward, one of the premiere professional learning organizations in the world, recognizes this need and has created seven *Standards for Professional Learning* (2011) in response. Their mission and request is that we, as readers, thinkers, learners, leaders, and educators, engage with these standards to guide our practice as we strive to meet unique contextual needs. It is a pleasure and honor to write this opening chapter to shed light on Learning Forward's important new Learning Designs standard. We must continue to prioritize professional learning as a catalyst to school and district improvement. This Designs standard helps us to prioritize learning designs and to understand how to effectively support learning and improvement.

For many years, I have had the privilege of facilitating professional learning opportunities that focus on helping school leaders of all kinds—teachers, principals, assistant principals, coaches, professional learning specialists, superintendents, deputy superintendents, and district leaders. Again and again these educators voice, in their concluding remarks, that their "prior training and education" always emphasized the importance of differentiating for children and adolescents. While they deeply value and appreciate that, they express that they also have become aware of how their training and education programs have unintentionally overlooked the importance of differentiating to support adult growth and learning. They remark that growing in their understanding of how to create conditions and supports for adult development, "energizes," "inspires" and "revitalizes" them. In fact, many have emphasized after workshops that understanding how to "differentiate" to support adult development, "gives hope." As one principal recently shared, "crafting effective learning environments is necessary for many reasons—including that they give us [principals] oxygen," and that, from her view enables us "to give more oxygen to our teachers" as we work to design effective learning environments for them.

We hope that this book and the others in this Learning Forward series, which illuminate the six other standards, will offer valuable resources for designing, implementing, and evaluating effective professional learning for educators in North America and abroad.

INTENTIONS FOR THIS CHAPTER: HOPES FOR YOU AND YOUR LEARNING

I have two primary goals for your learning in reading this chapter. First, I will do my best to introduce you to the Learning Designs standard itself and the three BIG IDEAS—or threads—that comprise it—namely (1) "apply learning theories, research and models," (2) "select . . . learning designs," and (3) "promot[e] . . . active engagement." This standard focuses on creating effective professional learning opportunities for all of us as educators that can increase our "effectiveness and results for all students." Learning Forward's Designs standard offers valuable components for us to consider within each of the strands composing this standard. As such, there are a variety of ways to design learning spaces for adults that align with this powerful standard. My second purpose is to offer a few examples from my own practice of facilitating professional learning to illustrate how I design learning opportunities for educators which align with the three big ideas of this standard. I offer these examples in case they are useful to you and with the understanding that that there are many alternatives to actualizing these bigger threads—strands—in practice.

One way I have been thinking about this standard and its strands or larger components is to envision each strand as a crucial perspective to consider that will enable you to meet adults where they are, to differentiate learning depending on their needs, and to create conditions for effective professional learning. You may find it useful to think of these strands as pools or containers that can be filled with many different theories and practices to design even more effective learning environments for adults. The way in which I, personally, implement—or fill—each of these strands, pools or containers is *one way—not the way.*

WHAT DO WE KNOW ABOUT EFFECTIVE PROFESSIONAL LEARNING? "IT'S LIKE OXYGEN!"

"[Effective professional learning]—it's like oxygen! I need it to grow and really, I need it to breathe. I also need it so that I can give more to others. It helps me to support my teachers' development."

Practicing High School Principal

Recently, I had the honor of facilitating a daylong professional learning experience for principals, assistant principals, district-level leaders, and teacher leaders. This particular workshop focused on some of the ideas you will learn about in this chapter: adult development, practices we can employ to support adult learning and development, and the importance of self-renewal. Toward the end of the day, one of the principals shared the comment quoted above about his realization about the importance of participating in effective learning opportunities. "It's like oxygen"—he offered and reflected aloud about how *he needs it—and so do his teachers.* This chapter and book offer ideas, practices, and strategies for you as a *designer of learning spaces for adults* and also for you as a learner in professional learning situations.

What do we know about the relationship between adult learning and student achievement? Well, we know that supporting adult growth and professional learning makes schools better places for children and adults (Darling-Hammond, Meyerson, LaPointe, & Orr, 2009; Donaldson, 2008; Fullan, 2005; Kegan & Lahey, 2009). We also know that there is a direct and positive relationship between supporting adult learning and increasing student achievement (Guskey, 1999; Moller & Pankake, 2006; Wagner, 2007). Yet as many of us have experienced, not all professional learning initiatives have the same effect on adults, nor do they have a positive effect on student achievement. In fact, recent research has confirmed what educators have long since understood—that strict content delivery during "more traditional professional development days" (or what is known in some circles as "sit and get" learning) has very little influence on teacher practice or student performance (Murnane & Willett, 2011).

However, Learning Forward's new Design standard helps us understand how we can create authentic professional learning opportunities that can make a positive and dramatic difference for adults, children, schools, and school systems. Indeed, thinking differently about how we design learning opportunities for educators can help us build internal capacity in schools and enhance student achievement. This is a giant step toward effectively meeting the many challenges that stand before us—and this urgent reframing sits at the heart of this book.

A developmental approach to advancing professional learning—which I will describe in greater detail in this chapter—is one promising way to help educators throughout the system build the internal capacities needed to meet the mounting adaptive challenges that define education today. We need to recognize the very real and important role that developmental diversity plays in professional learning, and we need to design and facilitate learning initiatives in ways that both honor and stretch this under-recognized form of diversity. Together, we can make a big difference with and for students, educators, and each other.

Before diving more deeply into the Learning Designs standard—and the promising ways it can inform professional learning today—I want to invite you to enjoy a brief "pause" moment. This pause is an opportunity to consider your own hopes for learning as you read this book, and your thoughts and experiences about professional learning. This is an invitation I often extend to educational leaders of all kinds at the beginning of workshops, seminars, and university courses that focus on supporting adult learning and development in schools, districts, and leadership preparation programs.

PLEASE PRESS YOUR PAUSE BUTTON

Double Clicking: Starting where you are?

This is an invitation for you to pause and take a few moments to reflect on the following questions before reading the rest of this chapter. I encourage you to consider these questions privately first and then with a colleague. You might find it helpful to reflect in writing.

1. What professional learning designs have you found most effective in supporting your own learning (e.g., oxygen)? Why did they work well for you?

2. What do you hope to learn about designing professional learning experiences that effectively support others' growth? In other words, what is one big take away you would like to get from reading this chapter?

CHAPTER OVERVIEW: ONE STANDARD, THREE DISTINCT AND INTERRELATED STRANDS

Integrating theories, research, and models of human learning into the planning and design of professional learning contributes to its effectiveness. Several factors influence decisions about learning designs, including the goals of the learning, characteristics of the learners, their comfort with the learning process and one another, their familiarity with the content, the magnitude of the expected change, educators' work environment, and resources available to support learning. The design of professional learning affects the quality and effectiveness.

Learning Forward, 2011, p. 40

In this chapter, I introduce the three strands of the Learning Designs standard: (1) *apply learning theories, research, and models*; (2) *select learning designs*; and (3) *promote active engagement*. The importance of these is summarized in the passage above. Intertwined with the discussion of each strand, I will present key elements of Robert Kegan's (1982, 1994, 2000) *constructive-developmental theory*, which helps us understand the qualitatively different ways that adults make sense of living, learning, teaching, and leading. In addition, I offer key practices, tips, and strategies derived from my research-based *models of learning-oriented school leadership and leadership development,* since these will help to bring the strands to life. As stated earlier, please remember that the examples, practices, and strategies offered herein are only some of the ways to think about bringing the standard to life.

Understanding constructive-developmental theory and my learning-oriented models (Drago-Severson, 2004b, 2009, 2012) are one promising way to reframe professional learning in alignment with Learning Forward's new standard. It is also one powerful way to integrate what we already know about effective professional learning *and* what is still possible. In light of this, and in addition to an overview of the Learning Designs standard, this chapter offers insight into a few of the myriad of ways to weave these strands together.

1. **Strand 1: Applying learning theories, research, and models.** This first strand concerns the way learning theories, research, and models can help us understand the adults we want to support. To differentiate our designs and implement them in effective ways, we must know how adults learn and how environments can meet them where they are in order to support their learning. I introduce constructive-developmental theory as an example of the "apply learning theories, research and models" strand. This theory sheds light on the different ways that adults make sense of the world and their work—and why this is important when designing professional learning experiences. More specifically, I will highlight the three different "ways of knowing" (or meaning-making systems) that are most common in adulthood—the *instrumental, socializing, and self-authoring.* Understanding these qualitatively different ways in which adults interpret their experiences can help facilitators of professional learning better craft contexts that meet adults where they are in a developmental sense, so learning initiatives can serve as effective *"holding environments"* for growth (Kegan, 1982, p. 115). While I circle back to this powerful framework throughout the chapter, I introduce it in relation to the first strand of the Learning Designs standard.

2. **Strand 2: Selecting learning designs.** The second strand builds upon empirical research and the differentiated processes and designs that adults need to learn and grow. To create meaningful designs, we must consider what processes offer the best supports and challenges to the adults we serve. I hope to achieve this by offering a brief overview of my learning-oriented models of school leadership (Drago-Severson, 2004b, 2009; Drago-Severson, Blum-DeStefano, & Asghar, 2013) and leadership development (Drago-Severson, 2012), including the four pillar practices, which can support the professional learning of adults with different ways of knowing. These pillars—*teaming, providing adults with leadership roles, collegial inquiry,* and *mentoring*—involve infusing traditional variations of these practices with developmental intentions, so they more effectively support adults with diverse needs at both the individual and group level. These models are offered as a way to bring the second two strands—select learning designs and promote active engagement—of the Learning Designs standard to life.

3. **Strand 3: Promoting active engagement.** The integration of the third strand brings the first two together for meaningful professional learning and emphasizes how the design does not stop when a "session" begins. In this section I offer tips about planning for professional development initiatives that involve the preparation that comes *before* the delivery of content, as well as the in-the-moment adjustments that get mapped out *during* facilitation. These strategies represent some of the best of what I've learned as a developmental psychologist and facilitator of adult learning over the past 25 years. These are shared as possible ways to connect to all three strands and the biggest intentions in Learning Designs standard.

I truly hope that this and all that is included in the other chapters in this book help you in your important and noble work of supporting adult learning and development in your own work context.

PLEASE PRESS YOUR PAUSE BUTTON

Double Clicking: What is important to you when designing learning for others and when participating in learning opportunities yourself?

This is another invitation to pause and take a few moments to reflect on the following questions before reading further. I invite you to consider these questions privately first and then with a colleague. You might find it helpful to reflect in writing.

1. What, from your perspective, constitutes a safe and productive learning space?

2. How, if at all, does your answer change, as you consider professional learning initiatives first as a *participant* and then as a *designer*?

3. What, in your view, are the critical components that need to be included when designing learning for other educators—whether in a team, in a faculty meeting, as a coach, and/or in offering professional learning days or initiatives?

REFRAMING "STANDARDS": DESIGNING EFFECTIVE PROFESSIONAL LEARNING THAT SUPPORTS ADULT GROWTH AND CAPACITY BUILDING

As standards become increasingly important to and for the practice of education today, it may be useful to pause and reflect about what standards *are*—and how they might help. What, for instance, can standards tell us about the positive things we are already doing in our practice? How might they point toward opportunities for continued improvement and growth? While these complex questions are beyond the scope of this chapter or even this book, it does strike me as particularly important that Learning Forward's new Learning Designs standard implicitly recognizes the complexity of facilitating adult learning and offers a call to do things even more effectively.

I have learned that facilitating this work—shaping growth enhancing conditions in professional learning environments—does not follow a specific blueprint or concrete steps. Nevertheless, there are certain things that we know and do that help us to increase our personal and organizational capacities and resources—and better meet the adaptive challenges that we face every day. In other words, in today's complex, ever-changing world, filled with enormous and new kinds of implicit and explicit demands, there is a vital need to carefully consider how we can *best* design learning environments that are supportive of growth. I define growth as increases in our cognitive, emotional or affective, intrapersonal (the way the self relates to the self), and interpersonal (the way the self relates to others) capacities that enable us to manage the complexities of leading, teaching, learning and living (Drago-Severson, 2004b, 2009, 2012).

More specifically, the three strands of this Learning Designs standard—(1) apply learning theories, research, and models; (2) select learning designs; and (3) promote active engagement—point toward the promise of crafting professional learning opportunities that invite educators to learn about content, learn by engaging with each other, and *learn from the process of learning itself.* This, I feel, is the heart of this work—and why this new standard is so important.

Below, I introduce each of the standard's three strands, augmenting the discussion with developmental principles and strategies that can help to bring each strand to life in practice.

Strand 1: Apply Learning Theories, Research, and Models

Cognitive psychologists, neuroscientists, and educators have studied how learning occurs for nearly a century. The resulting theories, research, and models of human learning shape the underlying framework and assumptions educators use to plan and design professional learning. While multiple designs exist, many have common features. . . .

Learning Forward, 2011, p. 40

The first strand of the Learning Designs standard focuses on the underlying beliefs and values that drive professional learning, and the common features of robust learning environments that are informed by theories, research, and models. For example, the strand names "active engagement, modeling, reflection, metacognition, application, feedback, ongoing support, and formative and summative assessment" as key components of effective learning designs (Learning Forward, 2011, p. 40).

PLEASE PRESS YOUR PAUSE BUTTON

Double Clicking: What is important to you?

Before reading more, please consider this invitation to pause and reflect on the following questions. I invite you to consider these questions privately first and then to discuss your responses with a colleague. You might find it helpful to reflect in writing.

1. When designing learning in your context, which theories, research, and models do you use to inform your design?

2. What, based on your experience, as either designer of learning or participant in learning environments, do you think are central components of effective learning designs?

The components listed at the start of this section are all very important. My approach and perspective, for example, have been informed and enriched primarily by constructive-developmental theory (Kegan, 1982, 1994, 2000), a neo-Piagetian theory of adult development created by Harvard psychologist Robert Kegan. Kegan's theory sheds light on how adults make meaning at a given point *and* over time, and how our ways of knowing can stretch and grow to be more complex if we are offered developmentally appropriate supports and challenges. While there is great promise in this premise in general—that adulthood can be a time of robust personal development rather than a fixed end-point—it is also particularly important for the design of professional learning opportunities.

For example, understanding that adults have different ways of knowing—or ways of taking things in, making sense of them, and putting them together—reminds us that we need to employ a variety of pedagogical practices when facilitating professional learning initiatives. Doing so enables us to both adequately meet adult learners—who have different ways of understanding their experiences—where they are (i.e., support) and to offer developmentally appropriate challenges or stretching (in a psychological sense) in order to support their learning and growth. In other words, what feels like a good fit pedagogically for one learner might feel overly challenging for another, so paying careful attention to the "goodness of fit" and the expectations we convey in designing learning opportunities can make a big difference for educators and for our schools. This strand emphasizes these big and important ideas as well.

To provide a little more context, it might be helpful to understand that constructive-developmental theory is based on three central principles: (1) constructivism, (2) developmentalism, and (3) what is referred to as the subject-object balance or meaning making system. I will explain these key principles next.

Constructivism, the first principle, sheds light on the fact that as human beings we *actively construct or make sense of* experiences— every minute of every day. In other words, the ways in which we interpret what we see and hear and experience is qualitatively different from person to person, and has a big influence on our understandings and perspectives. The second principle, *developmentalism,* highlights the promising notion that the way we make meaning of our experiences can become bigger and more encompassing over time—that we can, in fact, continue to develop and grow throughout the lifespan. Professional learning environments can help us to do this. The third major principle is what Kegan (1982) refers to as the *subject-object balance.* A person's way of knowing or meaning making system hinges on this balance. More specifically, this balance is a system that centers on the relationship between what we can have a perspective on and control (i.e., hold as "object") and what we cannot see about ourselves or others (i.e., are "subject to" or identified with). In essence, this third principle is really *all about what we can have perspective on and what we are blind to and cannot have perspective on.* The more perspective we can have on ourselves, others, and our relationships, the better we are able to manage complexity and also give back to others.

While Kegan's (1982, 1994, 2000; Kegan et al., 2001) constructive-developmental theory is composed of six qualitatively different stages or meaning making systems, research suggests that adults today most commonly make meaning with one of three ways of knowing—which I refer to as the instrumental, socializing, or self-authoring (Drago-Severson, 2004b, 2009, 2012). Like other, more recognized forms of diversity, one's way of knowing is an important facet of who one is at any given point in time. In other words, a person's way of knowing dictates and shapes beliefs about what constitutes effective help, successful practice, good teaching, effective leadership, and the necessary supports and challenges in order to learn and grow. Moreover, a person's way of knowing is not random. Rather, it is stable and consistent for a period of time and reflects a coherent system of logic. While context, of course, matters, a way of knowing might feel more like the way we *are* rather than something we *have* (Drago-Severson, 2004a, 2004b, 2009, 2012; Drago-Severson, Blum-DeStefano, & Asghar, 2013; Kegan, 1982, 1994).

Accordingly, a developmental approach to designing and facilitating professional learning takes into account adults' different ways of knowing. Thus, it helps us to shape learning experiences to be safe and productive "holding environments" (Kegan, 1982, p. 115) that support educators with different orientations—or ways of knowing, as I refer to them—and expectations. The concept of a *holding environment* was first described in the 1960s by pediatrician and psychoanalyst D. W. Winnicott. Kegan later used the term in his theory of adult development and maintained that we all need multiple forms of "holding" throughout our lives. His theory highlights that we must benefit from differentiated forms of "holding"—meaning support, nourishment, and care—in order to grow. Thus, Kegan's (1982) work extends Winnicott's (1965) definition of a holding environment to include the kinds of environments and relationships that provide opportunities for personal growth throughout the lifespan.

To better understand how to think about and shape these kinds of holding environments in designing professional learning for educators, I will discuss the three most common ways of knowing in adulthood—the instrumental, socializing, and self-authoring. In addition, I offer strategies for supporting and stretching (in the developmental sense) adults with different ways of knowing independently and collectively. Before turning to these ways of knowing, however, it is important to remember a few important facts. First, as you know, *development* is not the same as *intelligence.* In fact, a person can be very intelligent—as well as kind and caring—and make meaning with *any one of the three ways of knowing* discussed next. Second, each way of knowing has developmental strengths and limitations. Last, a particular way of knowing is not necessarily better than another. Rather, it depends on the fit between personal (internal) capacities and environmental demands. That said, the demands of contemporary education, and especially the adaptive challenges that we encounter every day, are calling for greater internal capacities. Therefore, designing learning experiences that help adults to understand, identify, and expand their ways of knowing is one promising way to improve schools and school systems together.

The instrumental way of knowing. Educators—and all adults for that matter—who make meaning with an instrumental way of knowing have a "what do you have that can help me—what do I have that can help you" orientation to their work, their teaching, their learning, their relationships, and the world. Importantly, instrumental knowers understand that observable events have realities separate from their own, but generally understand the world in very concrete (dualistic) terms. In light of this, instrumental knowers orient strongly toward rule following and feel supported when others provide specific, explicit advice to help them navigate decisions and responsibilities. These knowers can be caring and loving—though in a concrete manner (i.e., they expressed their care in a concrete manner). A limitation to this way of knowing is the inability to take others' perspectives fully (i.e., to stand in someone shoes). To best support and challenge these knowers, professional learning experiences need to offer a deliberate balance of clear structure and safe, collaborative opportunities and chances to look beyond the "one right way" of doing things and consider multiple perspectives and multiple alternative solutions.

The socializing way of knowing. Educators with a socializing way of knowing have more complex (internal) developmental capacities for reflection and the capacity to consider and reflect on other people's perspectives and actions. Unlike instrumental knowers, socializing knowers can think abstractly (in the psychological sense rather than the mathematical sense). Their orientation is other-focused, and such adults often subordinate their own needs to those of others. Interpersonal conflict is almost always experienced as a threat to the self, and acceptance by authorities and/or valued others is of the highest importance. When supporting the growth of socializing knowers, facilitators of professional learning can create opportunities for these adults to voice their own opinions before adopting those of valued others. Often, it is helpful to invite and encourage socializing knowers to share their perspectives in pairs or small groups prior to large group discussions. This helps them clarify their own beliefs, values, and standards before addressing a larger audience.

The self-authoring way of knowing. Adults with a self-authoring way of knowing generate their own internal value systems and author their own standards (Drago-Severson, 2006a, 2006b, 2007). They can identify abstract values, principles, and longer-term purposes and are able to prioritize and integrate competing values. These knowers can assess other people's expectations, standards, and judgments and compare them to their own. They have the capacity to reflect on and regulate interpersonal relationships but are not able to have perspective on their own self-system (ideology), since they are so closely identified with it. Like other adults, educators with a self-authoring way of knowing can be both supported and challenged through professional learning. While they will likely welcome opportunities to lead or express their values and beliefs, they can also benefit from gentle challenges to let go of their own perspectives and embrace opposing points of view.

Table 1.1 offers a concise overview of developmentally-appropriate supports and challenges that can be built into any professional learning initiative to support adults with each of these three most common ways of knowing.

As I will discuss in greater detail in the next section, the strategies offered in Table 1.1 can be built into any of the four pillar practices for growth—teaming, providing adults with leadership roles, collegial inquiry, and mentoring—which can help make professional learning initiatives become developmental "holding environments" for adults with different *ways of knowing.*

By way of example, and to further connect these ideas to the Learning Designs standard, it might be helpful to think about what it means—from a developmental perspective—to give and receive "feedback." A very important part of learning, feedback means different things to different people—and this standard reminds us of the importance of *differentiating* our feedback to adults with different ways of understanding and experiencing learning environments and the world. It also helps us to be mindful of the need to integrate a diversity of pedagogical practices and processes to enhance learning, in order to meet the needs of adults with different ways of knowing. (For a fuller discussion of feedback from a developmental perspective, please see Drago-Severson & Blum-DeStefano, forthcoming in 2015.)

Table 1.1 Developmentally Oriented Supports and Challenges for Facilitating Growth in Adults With Different Ways of Knowing

	Supports	*Challenges (Growing Edge)*
Instrumental Knowers	• Setting clear goals and expectations—especially when collaborating with colleagues and in professional learning situations (e.g., teaming, small group work) • Creating ground rules to guide conversations when engaging in learning • Providing explicit step-by-step procedures for dialogue and working with other colleagues, as well as explicit, concrete directions for working on tasks • Sharing examples of rules, purposes, and goals, as well as models of effective practices and/or examples of best practices • Offering ideas about how to share best practices with colleagues • Creating spaces in learning environments for these adults to engage in dialogue that centers on learning from concrete advice, specific skills, and information and instructions about how to improve instructional practice—including best practice models	• Creating opportunities—in general and in professional learning environments—for these adults to learn about and from multiple perspectives through the process of engaging in dialogue • Inviting these adults to engage in tasks that require abstract thinking (in the psychological sense) and helping instrumental knowers through the process. Protocols and instructions with clear goals and set timing are helpful • Encouraging movement beyond one "correct" solution and toward other possible, viable ways of proceeding. Creating conditions to learn from alternative perspectives—and modeling the process of doing this for these adult learners • Explicitly discussing how multiple perspectives can build abstract thinking and broaden perspective on self, others, and the relationships among them—in professional learning initiatives and in general (e.g., teams)

	Supports	Challenges (Growing Edge)
Socializing Knowers	• Ensuring that these educators feel known and accepted • Feeling that authorities and valued others confirm, acknowledge, and accept these knowers' own beliefs and encouraging them to voice their own beliefs and perspectives • Supervisors, valued colleagues and/or loved ones show acceptance • Providing opportunities for these educators to share perspectives in pairs or smaller groups *before* sharing with larger groups • Ensuring and modeling that interpersonal relationships are not jeopardized when differences of opinion arise • Modeling productive engagement with conflict	• Providing opportunities to develop one's own beliefs and becoming less dependent on others' approval • Encouraging these knowers to construct their own values and standards independently, and move away from co-constructing them • Support and model the acceptance of conflicting points of view without feeling threatened • Supporting these knowers in separating their own feelings and responsibilities from another person's • Supporting these knowers in distinguishing their own perspective from their need to be accepted
Self-Authoring Knowers	• Providing opportunities to learn about diverse points of view • Offering opportunities to analyze and critique ideas • Creating learning situations wherein these adults can explore their own goals • Ensuring that learning from the process takes place—and modeling this • Supporting learning about and demonstrating one's own competencies • Providing opportunities to critique one's own practices and vision • Emphasize competency • Offering leadership roles • Inviting demonstration of competencies and dialogue	• Challenging (stretching) these knowers to let go of their own perspective and embrace diametrically opposing alternatives • Supporting these knowers in accepting diverse problem-solving approaches that differ from their own • Challenging these educators to set aside their own standards for practice and open up to others' values and standards • Encouraging these educators to accept and learn from diverse ways to explore problems

Source: Adapted from Drago-Severson (2009); Drago-Severson, Blum-DeStefano, & Asghar (2013).

17

Some adults, for instance (e.g., self-authoring knowers), might welcome concise, direct feedback on their practice—as well as the opportunity to voice their own opinions and perspectives in return. Others, however (e.g., socializing knowers), might have a harder time taking in critical feedback if it is not expressed in a way that feels genuinely supportive, caring, and appreciative of that adult's positive contributions as well. Yet still others (e.g., instrumental knowers) might prefer more concrete feedback offered within a predetermined structure. Nevertheless, when offering feedback as a support to another adult's professional learning and growth (e.g., as part of a mentoring or supervisory relationship), it is important to remember that the most effective holding environments meet adults where they are in a developmental sense (i.e., recognize and respect their developmental needs and preferences), and also gently encourage these adults to stretch beyond comfortable competencies and capacities over time.

In the end, both constructive-developmental theory and the first strand of the Learning Designs standard illuminate the critical importance of infusing our learning designs with the best of what we know from theory, research, and models. Like you, I understand that there are many possible and promising theories, research, and models to draw from when shaping spaces as genuine learning contexts for self and others. Constructive-developmental theory is one example of a theory that can be employed when designing learning experiences for adults. As such, it offers a number of key, unique takeaways that have important implications for designers and facilitators of learning. I will leave you with these before turning next to the second strand of the standard:

- First, understanding developmental diversity can positively inform our design of effective professional learning environments and can assist with capacity building. Educators, like all adults, need *different supports* and *challenges to grow.* Table 1.1 illustrates some of the ways in which we can build these into our learning designs.
- A developmental vocabulary also enables us to move away from labeling adults based on behaviors—and toward better understanding how to support adult and leadership development in general, and especially in professional learning initiatives.

- Finally, considering the *developmental match* between one's expectations and adults' internal capacities to meet them will help professional learning leaders and facilitators shape contexts and opportunities that effectively support adult development at both the group and individual levels.

Our most important learnings come not simply when we see the world anew, but specifically when we see ourselves—and our role in creating the world—anew.

Ursula Versteegen

Strand 2: Selecting Learning Designs

If you get, give. If you learn, teach.

Maya Angelou

They may forget what you said but they will never forget how you made them feel.

Carl W. Buechner

We know that adults need to learn and grow in order to meet the pressing adaptive challenges they face as educators. Professional learning, then, needs to support and challenge educators to build their internal capacities. As we know, preparing for this involves great care and intentionality when designing learning initiatives for one's own and others' growth. In other words, we need to think carefully and deliberately about differentiation and goodness of fit (in a developmental sense) when selecting and planning a design. As this strand of the Learning Designs standard states:

When choosing designs for professional learning, educators consider multiple factors. The first is the intended outcome, drawn from analysis of student and educator learning needs. Learning designs that engage adult learners in applying the processes they are expected to use facilitate the learning of those behaviors by making them more explicit. Effective designs for professional learning assist educators in moving beyond comprehension of the surface features of a new idea or practice to developing a more complete understanding of its purposes, critical attributes, meaning, and connection to other approaches. (Learning Forward, 2011, pp. 41–42)

As the above passage indicates, this strand of the standard—which focuses on *selecting* learning designs—points to the importance of

- The *intentionality* behind the choices we make as designers of learning (i.e., designing learning opportunities that draw from what we know from theory and research to explicitly teach about and model growth-enhancing practices),
- Selecting structures and practices that can support diverse learners at both the group and individual levels (e.g., the pillar practices—teaming, providing leadership roles, engaging in collegial inquiry, and mentoring), and
- Carefully and thoroughly planning and preparing when facilitating and leading learning (e.g., allocating time, balancing diverse activities, and making your plans, thinking, and actions transparent for learners so that they can (a) deepen their learning, (b) develop a more comprehensive understanding of its "purposes, critical attributes, meaning, and connection to other approaches," and (c) apply learning in real time).

PLEASE PRESS YOUR PAUSE BUTTON

Double Clicking: How are you intentional in your designs?

Before reading more, please consider this invitation to pause and reflect on the following questions. I invite you to consider these questions privately first and then to discuss your responses with a colleague or two. You might find it helpful to reflect in writing.

1. What factors do you consider when selecting learning designs in your work context?

2. How do you feel they are working? What, if anything, would you like to improve?

As I will describe in greater detail below, these ideas resonate with what I've learned over the past two decades about the importance of developmental intentionality, or the careful crafting of safe and productive spaces when facilitating learning opportunities that support adults' learning, development, and internal capacity building. Indeed, as facilitators of any professional learning experience, we are all learning designers in one sense or another. Moreover, it is always important when designing learning opportunities to consider how participants' ways of knowing will influence their experiences (this was emphasized in relation to the first strand and, as mentioned there, it is something we can care for when consider the other two strands as well).

Toward this end, *intentionality of design* involves deliberately selecting and employing a variety of instructional approaches to meet adults where they are developmentally—and voicing this aloud as a show of respect and transparency (for a further discussion of this, see Drago-Severson, 2012). As a wise teacher of mine once explained during a graduate course years ago, "I'm going to use a variety of practices to support your learning. Please remember that what you love, the person sitting right next to you might not find as meaningful as you do!" It is indeed true that intentionally selecting diverse practices for your learning designs—and explaining the rationale behind these decisions to participants—can help educators get the most out of your time together, and can also help learners understand how and why to employ similar strategies in their own contexts. This sits at the heart of the *Select Learning Design* strand.

Before describing some of the ideas related to planning and selecting effective learning designs, we should consider the four pillar practices for growth—teaming, providing adults with leadership roles, collegial inquiry, and mentoring—which constitute my learning-oriented model of school leadership (Drago-Severson, 2004b, 2009) and also play key roles in my learning-oriented model of leadership development (Drago-Severson, 2012). I discuss these here because they are intimately related to the Learning Designs standard.

In fact, longitudinal research has shown that *experiencing* these practices—which involves deliberately reframing traditional collaborative practices with developmental intentions—while *in the process* of learning about them can serve as an important support to educator learning and growth, and can also have a positive and lasting influence on practice (Drago-Severson, Blum-DeStefano & Asghar, 2013). By looking beyond the delivery of specific content (which is of course important) to the structures we employ to meet the needs of learners, we can more effectively shape professional learning initiatives as supports to individual, school, and system-wide growth—and student achievement.

Teaming. While you may already be familiar with or have personally experienced the practice of teaming (it is, arguably, the most common form of collaborative work employed in schools and districts today), a developmental approach to teaming involves intentionally inviting adults to question their own and other people's assumptions—together. Rather than collaborating simply to complete a task or address a problem (which does, of course, still happen), the pillar practice of teaming also emphasizes the importance of creating a safe space in which to experiment with one's thinking—and provides opportunities for collaborative decision-making and reflection. As such, teaming can be a powerful choice for professional learning initiatives geared toward the generation of new ideas, solutions, questions, and programs, among other things.

Of course, adults with different ways of knowing will experience teaming differently, so it is important when employing teaming as part of a learning design to recognize and scaffold these different forms of participation. When considering how to differentiate supports and challenges within team structures, it might be helpful to review some of the information in Table 1.1—and consider how to integrate components for adults with each of the three most prevalent ways of knowing. It is often helpful to set norms or ground rules about voicing opinions, as this could feel risky for some individuals for different reasons. Instrumental knowers, for instance, will need support to be able to consider multiple perspectives. Socializing knowers could initially find it uncomfortable to share their thoughts and observations if others disagree, especially when conflict emerges. These adults would need encouragement over time to understand that conflict can help develop more effective solutions to dilemmas. In contrast, learning from dialogue and conflict could be experienced as stimulating to self-authoring knowers. Nevertheless, encouraging these adults to consider opposing perspectives would support their growth over time. Discussing hopes, expectations, and requests for supports with colleagues beforehand (i.e., setting norms and ground rules), then, can help adults recognize their different orientations to voicing opinions in the group, and can help make teams more authentic learning spaces or holding environments for participants.

Providing leadership roles. By assuming leadership roles, adults share power and decision-making authority. Leadership roles are opportunities to raise not only one's consciousness but also a community's consciousness. These roles enable adults to benefit from each other's expertise and knowledge. However, unlike the commonly used term "distributive leadership," the pillar practice of providing adults with leadership roles involves intentionally offering these roles with an eye toward supporting and challenging the new leader's growth—or growing edge (developmentally speaking). In other words, rather than simply assigning tasks, *providing leadership roles* deliberately offers developmental supports and challenges to educators who are assuming leadership roles, in order to help them negotiate the oft-competing demands and complexities inherent in such roles while they exercise leadership, attend to their practice, and work to assist with larger school or systemic needs.

Just as with teaming, however, leadership roles will be perceived and experienced differently by different adults depending upon their way of knowing. For instance, those who are challenged by assuming authority (i.e., instrumental and socializing knowers) might initially require considerable support as they take on leadership. Self-authoring knowers, as you know, are adults who have enhanced internal capacities and look to themselves to generate values and standards when exercising leadership. These adults will feel supported by having the opportunity to put their ideas into action when assuming leadership roles. Regardless of one's way of knowing, leadership roles can serve as effective holding environments when those providing the role offer appropriate supports and challenges. This way, experiences can be used—not simply as additional responsibilities or ways to distribute workload demands but also as intentionally crafted opportunities for growing and learning.

Collegial inquiry. Collegial inquiry is a special, developmental type of reflective practice that involves learning with and from others by engaging in dialogue together. While reflective practice—which has increasingly become an indispensable part of educators' everyday practice—can be done in isolation, collegial inquiry involves purposefully reflecting on one's assumptions in dialogue with one or more partners as part of the learning process. Collegial inquiry provides opportunities to develop more complex perspectives by thinking with and listening to others. Many educators engage in collegial inquiry to enhance reflection, share in decision-making, and enhance professional learning. Examples include

- Reflecting privately, in writing, in response to questions or prompts, and then discussing ideas with others,
- Exploring case-based dilemmas and scenarios to apply learning, improve instructional practice, and gain insight into their own thinking, and
- Engaging in the process of collaborative goal setting.

As educators consider new and evolving pedagogy, curricula, standards, student work, and future paths during professional learning initiatives and other contexts, opportunities for group reflection and dialogue will support growth and capacity building. However, as we know, and just as is the case with the other pillar practices, carefully setting the context for and creating the conditions that support genuine collegial inquiry is essential.

Mentoring. As one of the oldest ways of supporting adult development, mentoring has been around for thousands of years and has taken many forms. From a developmental perspective, however, the pillar practice of mentoring intentionally creates opportunities for broadening perspectives, examining assumptions, and sharing expertise. It can be employed in numerous contexts and relationships, including pairing expert professionals with other adults, pairing veterans with deep knowledge of a school's mission with new community members, and group or team mentoring.

It is now generally accepted that no single mentoring relationship can meet *all* of a person's needs for growth. In fact, research shows that the most successful mentoring relationships are nested in a larger developmental set of connections (Higgins, Chandler, & Kram, 2007; McGowan, Stone, & Kegan, 2007). There is general agreement that we need mentors throughout our lives, as well as recognition that our needs for support and challenges from mentors change as we grow. Moreover, as with the three other pillars, effective mentoring relationships need to offer a balance of support, challenge, and continuity that are aligned with a person's way of knowing to best support growth.

In summary, the ways in which we engage in all four of the pillar practices—or any form of learning or collaborative work—varies according to our way of knowing. With appropriate support and challenges, we can grow and participate in these processes and our school environments more effectively. Moreover, it is important to note that these pillars can be used individually or in combination, as robust developmental structures for building internal capacity. This is especially important to understand when selecting practices and elements to include in professional learning designs of any kind—including workshops, seminars, developmental institutes, long-term learning opportunities, and everyday practice—because each pillar practice can support the learning and growth of diverse individuals simultaneously.

A few thoughts about the importance of planning. When selecting a pillar practice or learning design, the second strand of Learning Forward's new Learning Designs standard reminds us of the critical importance of behind-the-scenes planning. Effective design, after all, is not just about selecting a particular pillar or learning experience, but also carefully considering ahead of time the different activities you would like to incorporate, and also how long you realistically expect each component to take. Thinking carefully about the time educators would need to complete an activity—like finding partners for a pair-share or reflecting privately in journals before collegial inquiry, or reporting back to the group about discussions during teaming—is essential when designing the flow of a session.

Mapping out the time in this way is largely about balance—about differentiating modes and activities in ways that meet the developmental needs of participants with diverse ways of knowing. Yet, it is also about *transparency,* because explaining—as you're introducing them—the kinds of things learners will be discussing and doing throughout the shared time helps keep everybody on the same page, creates a shared expectation for the professional learning experience, and models the importance of being explicit. More specifically, explaining the timing and developmental intention behind design decisions helps to provide an aerial—or balcony—view for learners—as they simultaneously learn about and experience a developmental approach to supporting adult growth. Doing so can also help them translate these practices back in their own work contexts.

Happiness is neither virtue nor pleasure nor this thing nor that but simply growth. We are happy when we are growing.

Attributed to William Butler Yeats

Strand 3: Promoting Active Engagement

Active engagement in professional learning promotes change in educator practice and student learning. Active engagement occurs when learners interact during the learning process and with one another.

Learning Forward, 2011, pp. 41–42

This Learning Designs strand—promoting active engagement—emphasizes that creating conditions within professional learning environments for educators to collaborate "consistently produces strong, positive effects on achievement of learning outcomes" (Learning Forward, 2011, p. 42). This highlights the importance of respecting "adults and professionals" and of giving educators "significant voice and choice in shaping their own learning" (p. 42). The ideas presented in this strand are intimately connected to those in the first and second strands. In other words, we need to consistently consider how to promote *active engagement* while thinking carefully about (a) how to design learning (strand #2) and (b) how to use theories of learning, research related to learning and adult development, and models to support learning (strand #1). In effect, all three strands are inextricably linked at a fundamental level.

This strand also reminds us of the importance of creating opportunities within professional learning environments for educators to "construct personal meaning of their learning" through *active learning processes,* which include: "discussion and dialogue, writing, demonstrations, inquiry, reflection, metacognition, co-construction of knowledge, practice with feedback, coaching, modeling and problem solving" (p. 42). By promoting active learning processes and by creating opportunities for educators to explore both their individual and collective sense making and experiences, adult learners have the space to actively construct meaning, and "analyze, evaluate and synthesize" pre-existing and new knowledge and more effective practices.

The act of designing learning and differentiating is an ongoing process that we need to consider before, during, and after facilitating a learning experience for other adults. As such, it requires a constant weaving together of all three strands in the Learning Designs standard.

PLEASE PRESS YOUR PAUSE BUTTON

Double Clicking: What is important to you in terms of active engagement?

Once again, and before reading further, please consider this invitation to pause and reflect on the following questions. I invite you to consider these questions privately first and then to share with a colleague. You might find it helpful to reflect in writing.

1. What are the kinds of experiences that enable you to actively engage when in a professional learning situation?

2. What kinds of practices and structures do you build into professional learning environments to help other adults engage with material, processes, and each other? How do you think they are working for others? For you?

This third strand of the Learning Designs standard—promoting active engagement—speaks to a number of key aspects of in-the-moment facilitation of professional learning. An extension of employing theory, incorporating structures to support learning, as well as planning and promoting active engagement involves

1. Giving adults _choice_ in their learning and harnessing the power of working collaboratively with others,

2. Flexibility and sensitivity as a facilitator, or a feeling of being "in tune" with your audience and their rhythm and energy levels in order to best serve and meet their needs, and

3. The realization that modeling and self-knowledge speak volumes about who we are as facilitators of adult learning—and are essential for building trust.

Below, I discuss each of these three big ideas, and also wisdom from educators from whom I've had the honor to learn in my research and workshops around the globe.

A few thoughts about differentiation and collaboration. The third strand's emphases on promoting active engagement by inviting adults into "discussion and dialogue, writing, demonstrations, inquiry, reflection, metacognition, co-construction of knowledge, practice with feedback, coaching, modeling, and problem solving" all point to the promise and power of *differentiation*—and to the momentous progress we can make when we commit to learning with, from, and for each other.

For example, and in case helpful, when facilitating professional learning experiences of any kind, I intentionally incorporate multiple kinds of modalities and opportunities for adult learners to engage in collaborative work into the design, including

- Private time for educators to think, through journaling (writing) and/or reflection, followed by opportunities to discuss ideas with another person or in a small group,
- Application exercises that invite educators to translate theories and ideas to their own practice in small groups or teams,
- Quick instructor-led check-ins, and
- Invitations to share ideas with larger or whole groups.

Building in different opportunities for reflecting in writing and with colleagues can be supportive of growth and learning—both in single-day professional learning experiences and in events that take place over time. Moreover, opportunities to engage in free writing in response to prompts, questions, or big ideas can help to create spaces for individuals regardless of their way of knowing. Balancing these opportunities for dialogue is also important and intentional.

Still, promoting active engagement is not just about implementing the structures or activities above but employing them purposefully—with an eye toward differentiation and adjustment in order to meet needs of individuals and groups at any moment in time. After all, it is not just the structures we create, but the experiences we design within those structures for adult learners that make a difference to their learning. Attending carefully to developmental diversity as a facilitator is one important way that we can create environments of high support and challenge that can reach and connect and inspire learners with different needs, learning preferences, and ways of knowing. As you know, when we differentiate for students, we need to focus on process, product, and content (Tomlinson & McTighe, 2006), in addition to meeting them where they are. The Designs standard helps us understand better how to do the same for adults.

For example, when scaffolding reflection, I usually invite educators to engage with one other person whom they choose when sharing or discussing ideas. I'll often invite them to consider finding one person they do not know very well, and then give them a minute or two to select a partner. At other times, I've found that it can be helpful to invite educators to find two partners (triads) or engage in small groups of 4 (quads), depending upon the size of the group and the intention behind the reflection/discussion. I often close an activity by inviting educators to share anything they'd like to offer to the larger group. I've found that moving from the comfort of sharing with a partner or small group to more public reporting supports active engagement in professional learning contexts of all kinds.

It is also important when facilitating professional learning to make sure that participants feel safe in sharing across contexts. Indeed, colleagues and I have found that educators need to have a deep sense of safety *before* they can effectively engage in learning, and we view this feeling of trust and security as an essential *precondition* of learning (Drago-Severson, Blum-DeStefano, & Asghar, 2013). Developing a shared understanding of group norms and confidentiality can be a very powerful support to collaboration and engagement. In Figure 1.1, I share a protocol that I developed that can be used to help new and existing groups effectively establish norms. However, it is also important to remember that, should you decide to adopt this process, it is equally important that groups periodically check in about the norms they've established. This creates opportunities for individuals to add ideas to the discussion, and also for the group to (a) revisit norms, (b) discuss how they feel things have been going, and (c) make decisions about whether or not they want to modify or adjust norms to improve their collaborative work. Educators have explained that it is comforting to know that they will have chances to revisit and adjust norms and ground rules. Establishing norms together and revisiting them over time is another promising way to promote active engagement.

Figure 1.1   A Protocol for Establishing Norms and Ground Rules

While the amount of time is not included in the protocol below, it is wise to allocate specific amounts of time for each part of the process. For example, for a group of eight, I usually allow 15 minutes for initial introductions and 25 to 30 minutes for discussion of safe learning environment and confidentiality. Of course, times will vary depending on the number of team members. A general guideline for how to go about establishing team ground rules follows. I hope you find this useful.

1. Invite members to free write (i.e., write down what comes to mind without censoring) or free think for two to three minutes in response to the following two questions: What constitutes a safe, productive, and supportive group learning context for you? What makes a group learning space unsafe for you and your learning?

2. Before each group member has a chance to share—whatever he or she feels comfortable sharing with colleagues in the group— one member will want to volunteer to take notes on what is discussed, type up the notes, and provide copies for all group members. The idea here is not to capture every word verbatim but rather to capture the essence of what is said, with direct quotations when possible.

3. Invite group members to share their thinking with one another. Doing so helps to develop ground rules or norms for engaging in group discussion and for creating a safe learning environment. This is especially important because group members will often share their personal experiences of working with teams.

4. At the next group meeting, distribute the notes from the previous meeting so all members can add to them, if needed. Periodically revisiting this ground rule or shared norm document and checking in with group members about these important issues can strengthen collaboration and support learning and development.

5. After the safe and productive group learning environment discussion, if the topic hasn't come up already, the group will want to come to a shared understanding of what kind of confidentiality agreement they'd like to make. After the group has agreed how to manage confidentiality, the person who is taking notes will want to restate the agreement for the group and add it to the document, along with the group's thinking about what makes a safe and productive team learning environment. Group members will want to discuss how they want to handle confidentiality in terms of issues discussed in the group with others within the school, for instance.

Source: Adapted from Drago-Severson (2009), p. 93.

Thoughts related to flexibility and sensitivity. While it is essential to carefully plan for professional learning ahead of time, I have also learned that it is equally important to "go with the flow" when facilitating professional learning. In other words, being willing to adjust plans in the moment (even though this can sometimes be difficult) is key to meeting the needs of adult learners. Often, for example, in the middle of a session, I'll realize that a group has more questions about a topic than anticipated—or conversely, that they're ready to move on without additional discussion. Rather than forge ahead to successfully "finish" my original plan or schedule, I've learned that it is well worth it to adjust the schedule—just as you would when teaching children and youth.

This kind of flexibility involves the adjustments we as facilitators make in the moment—when we sense something is needed to enhance the experience or when something unanticipated is going on for learners. This, as you know, is really about paying attention to adults as learners. It's about respecting their pace, and it's about feeling the energy in the room. While we are in a room as facilitators, this kind of sensitivity is key. One way to think about this is that we—as facilitators and designers of learning experiences—need to be able to move back and forth from the "dance floor" (the doing) to the "balcony" (looking down on it). This helps to promote active engagement and learning.

Modeling and self-knowledge. Of course, this ability to have perspective on the events of a professional learning initiative is a capacity in and of itself—and one that can be acquired and practiced. Really, facilitating this kind of learning—like leadership in general—is a true gift of self, and one that requires a certain degree of modeling and self-knowledge. For example, I believe deeply that we need to be a *model* of what we are teaching. What we say is important, but what we *do* is even more important. Why? As you know, it's because our actions are what people pay attention to—whether one is a parent, a teacher leader, a school or district leader, a university professor, or a learning leader of any kind. Self-knowledge is a vital part of this process. In other words, we must know who we are and be comfortable with ourselves in order to create the most effective growing opportunities for others. As you might suspect, this is an ongoing process. The better we know ourselves, the better we are able to serve those in our care, and the better we can build holding environments and professional learning opportunities that pivot on inviting adults to actively engage with concepts and processes. Doing so supports the growth and internal capacity building of others.

How does one model who one is as a facilitator? What does this look like in practice? Perhaps an example here would be of help. I have thought a lot about the core values that inform my work as a facilitator of adult learning, and I have shared many of them with you throughout this chapter. I care deeply, for instance, about trust, respect, and collaboration, and about developmental intentionality in both leadership and professional learning. *Really listening* is one way that I try to model what I believe in across every context and each day. Perhaps more than anything, this listening stance invites and supports active engagement.

You can model genuine listening simply by the way you hold and carry yourself in a room. Being physically and psychologically present and unequivocally open to educators as they offer questions, insights, and ideas enables facilitators of professional learning to create safe contexts where learners are and feel respected and heard. Indeed, what we say, how we say it, how we respond, and the spaces we create for sharing can help learners to see and feel that we value and respect them—and their questions, ideas, feelings, presence, and growth. All of this works synergistically to promote active engagement.

We can demonstrate that we value, respect, and welcome learners and their questions and contributions in many ways. Below are a few practices that are often effective in promoting authentic engagement:

- Respond to educators' questions with positive affirmations, acknowledgements of their important questions, and offerings of sincere gratitude. I really feel that it is courageous to ask questions, share uncertainty, admit to not knowing something. It can make us feel vulnerable, I think. For example, I'll often say things like, *I appreciate your asking that. Thank you, that's a really important question. I'm so glad you asked.* And here's the most important part of this—it's, as you know, VERY important to feel it and mean it when I say it.
- Listen carefully to learners' questions and paraphrase them to make sure that you understand what was asked. This simultaneously helps a learner feel heard, and also helps to make sure that others in the room have heard the question.

- Invite participants in the room to respond to what's been shared—whether it is a personal reflection or a question.
- Give generous amounts of wait time.

A Few Closing Thoughts and Future Implications

Dreams are necessary to life.

Anais Nin

The trees give so that they may live, for to withhold is to perish.

Khalil Gibran

The ideas presented in Learning Forward's new Learning Designs standard are important, and they are a call for greater mindfulness and intentionality. Since we are all designers of learning, we know that in our work with colleagues, parents, and students, design has an important and powerful effect on learning. Recognizing, then—as this Learning Designs standard emphasizes—that aligning our designs with what we know about the different ways adults learn, and how they learn best, holds great promise for building capacity and improving schools, and for the future of education.

Learning Forward's decision to refer to what used to be called "professional development" as "professional learning" is significant, and so too is the commitment to sharing these new standards and ideas. In order to be effective, professional learning needs to feel meaningful and valuable to adult learners. Integrating theories, research, and models of human learning is a promising pathway for professional learning to achieve its intended outcomes—and to open enormous possibilities for growth.

This standard also suggests the promise in reframing the way we think about and label professional learning. While old-fashioned professional development or "PD" often took place in bounded sessions and at particular times (such as PD days, or during formal evaluations), the most effective professional learning is part of each and every day. As such, we need to think carefully about the kind of structures and learning opportunities that allow learning to seep out into the fabric of our collaborations and practice—to make our days and hearts permeable to learning with, for, and from one another in ways both formal and informal.

As technology advances, we are finding more ways to connect with each other across time and space. It is also true that some of the most important and meaningful learning can happen when we least expect it. Embracing the new possibilities for learning opens new horizons for growth and helps us catch a glimpse of what professional learning may look like in years to come.

Of course, at the heart of any professional learning initiative you will find the people who—together—are doing the learning, teaching, leading, and growing. If we do not care for each other—and ourselves—as we journey forward to meet the swelling tide of complex and demanding challenges heading our way, this work will not be possible. Just as we need to know ourselves to give our best to others, we need to refill and renew ourselves, too, or we will be left with little to give.

I end this chapter in the way it began, with hope and admiration. It's important to remember that it's often difficult to know the reach of your design work. You are making a difference—a difference each time you facilitate adult learning, regardless of context. I leave you with a wise thought to hold onto tightly.

Tamarind trees yield fruit for over two centuries.

Vandana Shiva

PLEASE PRESS YOUR PAUSE BUTTON

Double Clicking: What do you see as your BIG take aways?

Thank you for reading this chapter. I hope you found it useful. Before moving to the next chapters in this book, please consider this invitation to pause and reflect on your learning. I invite you to consider these questions privately first and then with a colleague or two. You might find it helpful to reflect in writing.

1. After reading this chapter, what stands out to you as three of your takeaways or lessons learned?

2. When you consider what you've learned about the Learning Designs standard and the three threads composing it—(1) apply

learning theories, research, and models—for example, ways of knowing; (2) select learning designs—for example, pillar practices; and (3) promote active engagement—for example, checking in or setting norms—what are some of the insights you have related to each of these threads? What, if any, ah-ha moments did you experience?

3. What are three action steps you will take after reading this chapter to enhance professional learning opportunities for others and for yourself? In other words, how do you think you will implement what you've learned?

4. What kinds of supports, if any, will you secure to help you with implementing these new insights in terms of enhancing learning designs in your work setting?

REFERENCES

Darling-Hammond, L., Meyerson, D., LaPointe, M., & Orr, T. (2009). *Preparing principals for a changing world: Lessons from effective school leadership programs.* San Francisco: Jossey-Bass.

Donaldson, G. A. (2008). *How leaders learn: Cultivating capacities for school improvement.* New York: Teachers College Press.

Drago-Severson, E. (2004a). *Becoming adult learners: Principles and practices for effective development.* New York: Teachers College Press.

Drago-Severson, E. (2004b). *Helping teachers learn: Principal leadership for adult growth and development.* Thousand Oaks: Corwin.

Drago-Severson, E. (2006a, Summer). Learning-oriented leadership: Transforming a school through a program of adult learning. *Independent School Journal,* 58–62.

Drago-Severson, E. (2006b, March). How can you better support teachers' growth? *The Learning Principal, 1*(6), 1, 6–7.

Drago-Severson, E. (2007). Helping teachers learn: Principals as professional development leaders. *Teachers College Record, 109*(1), 70–125.

Drago-Severson, E. (2009). *Leading adult learning: Supporting adult development in our schools.* Thousand Oaks: Corwin and Learning Forward.

Drago-Severson, E. (2012). *Helping educators grow: Strategies and practices for supporting leadership development.* Cambridge, MA: Harvard Education Press.

Drago-Severson, E., & Blum-DeStefano, J. (2015, forthcoming). *The art of feedback: Tell me so I can hear you.* Cambridge, MA: Harvard Education Press.

Drago-Severson, E., Blum-DeStefano, J., & Asghar, A. (2013). *Learning for leadership: Developmental strategies for building capacity in our schools.* Thousand Oaks: Corwin.

Drago-Severson, E., Maslin-Ostrowski, P., & Hoffman, A. (2013). In one voice: Aspiring and practicing school leaders embrace the need for a more integrated approach to leadership preparation and development. *International Journal for Adult Vocational Education and Technology* 4(4), 55–73.

Fullan, M. (2005). *Leadership and sustainability: Systems thinkers in action.* Thousand Oaks, CA, and Ontario, Canada: Corwin and the Ontario Principals' Center.

Guskey, T.R. (April 1999). *New Perspectives on Evaluating Professional Development.* Paper presented at the annual meeting of the American Educational Research Association, Montreal, Canada.

Heifetz, R. A. (1994). *Leadership without easy answers.* Cambridge, MA: Harvard University Press.

Higgins, M. C., Chandler, D. E., & Kram, K. E. (2007). Relational engagement and developmental networks. In B. Ragins & K. Kram (Eds.), *The handbook of mentoring at work: Research, theory, and practice* (pp. 349–372). Thousand Oaks, CA: Sage.

Kegan, R. (1982). *The evolving self: Problems and process in human development.* Cambridge, MA: Harvard University Press.

Kegan, R. (1994). *In over our heads: The mental demands of modern life.* Cambridge, MA: Harvard Press.

Kegan, R. (2000). What "Form" Transforms? A Constructive-Developmental Approach to Transformative Learning. In J. Mezirow & Associates (Eds.), *Learning As Transformation* (pp. 35–70). San Francisco: Jossey-Bass.

Kegan, R., Broderick, M., Drago-Severson, E., Helsing, D., Popp, N., & Portnow, K. (2001). *Toward a "new pluralism" in the ABE/ESOL classroom: Teaching to multiple "cultures of mind."* NCSALL [National Center for the Study of Adult Literacy and Learning] Research Monograph #19. Boston, MA: World Education.

Kegan, R., & Lahey, L. L. (2001). *How the way we talk can change the way we work: Seven languages for transformation.* San Francisco: Jossey-Bass/Wiley.

Kegan, R., & Lahey, L. L. (2009). *Immunity to change: How to overcome it and unlock the potential in yourself and your organization.* Boston: Harvard Business School Press.

Learning Forward (2011). *Standards for professional learning.* Oxford, OH: Author.

McGowan, E. M., Stone, E. M., & Kegan, R. (2007). A constructive-developmental approach to mentoring relationships. In B. R. Ragins & K. E. Kram (Eds.), *The mentoring handbook of mentoring at work: Theory, research and practice* (pp. 401–425). Thousand Oaks, CA: Sage.

Moller, G., & Pankake, A. (2006). *Lead with me: A principal's guide to teacher leadership.* Larchmont, NY: Eye On Education.

Murnane, R. J., & Willett, J. B. (2011). *Methods matter: Improving causal inference in educational and social science.* New York: Oxford University Press.

Tomlinson, C. A., & McTighe, J. (2006). *Integrating differentiated instruction and understanding by design: Connecting content and kids.* Alexandria, VA: ASCD [Association for Supervision and Development].

Wagner, T. (2007). Leading for change: Five 'habits of mind' that count. *Education Week, 26*(45), pp. 29, 32.

Wagner, T., Kegan, R., Lahey, L., Lemons, R. W., Garnier, J., Helsing, D., Howell, A., & Rasmussen, H. T. (2006). *Change leadership: A practical guide to transforming our schools.* San Francisco: Jossey-Bass/Wiley.

CHAPTER TWO

Learning Designs

The Bridge Between Planning and Implementation

Patricia Roy

> *. . . because teachers have such fine ability to learn, all currently used professional development models can succeed if properly implemented. . . . [V]arious models are good for various purposes and should not be compared based on a single criterion. None will get you everywhere you might want to go.*
>
> Joyce and Calhoun, 2010

In a large urban district in the South, I was helping school leaders learn about the professional learning standards. Participants read descriptions of two professional learning designs that focused on helping elementary teachers use a new inquiry-based science curriculum. The first scenario focused on helping educators understand the layout of the new curriculum, the resources available through the district and online, the benchmark testing schedule, and the difference between direct and inquiry-based instruction. The learning design was primarily lecture coupled with colorful graphics and interspersed with an occasional video. The second scenario shared the same goal but was filled with small group activities, discussion, a hands-on search of new materials, and planning and teaching a mini-lesson to another similar grade-level team. As the work group reflected on the differences and similarities between the two designs, a senior administrator summed up the difference succinctly: The second example clearly had implementation in mind.

Implementation is the ultimate purpose of using different professional learning designs—to assist and support educators in using new strategies that have been found to improve student learning. Merely having teachers "know" about new strategies is not enough; classroom use of new strategies is the component that will cause the desired impact on student learning. The ultimate goal in professional learning is improved student learning, but that occurs when educators actually put into practice new strategies, curriculum, and procedures in the classroom.

Imagine a picture of an iceberg—a small mound of shimmering white ice floating above water anchored by an enormous underwater foundation of dense blue glass. Learning designs, the most visible part of professional learning, function like that visible upper part of the iceberg. Learning designs include the activities we conduct, the conversations we have, the projects and planning that we typically refer to as "professional development." Underneath those observable events lies the foundation that undergirds the activities, defines its purpose and outcomes, and directs the implementation of new skills and strategies grounded in deep understanding and knowledge.

Many educators, from state departments and universities to districts and schools, believe that improving professional learning programs can be accomplished merely by identifying new learning strategies that transcend the ubiquitous workshop format. This belief is most likely grounded in the explosion of information about an assortment of learning designs, as well as research that found the traditional in-service day rarely influences long-term practice (Joyce & Showers, 2002).

New designs are important but even more critical is grounding the planning of professional learning in (1) analyzing student learning data, (2) identifying learning goals that align student needs with educator needs, and (3) identifying specific educator learning content, which might include content knowledge, pedagogy, learning theory, and classroom management. These diagnostic elements become the guidance systems for professional learning—clearly targeting a measurable, observable outcome for teachers and ultimately their students. These are the beginning elements of the cycle of continuous improvement introduced in the Learning Communities standard and the first volume of this series.

Professional learning mirrors other improvement efforts—analyzing student needs, setting clear and measurable goals, and clearly identifying the "what" or content of the plan is necessary *before* activities are identified and action plans created. Once we are clear about where we are going, then we can select the path to get us there. A new learning design will not necessarily result in improved educator learning if the underlying planning hasn't been adequately conducted.

Conversely, once thorough planning has been accomplished, the learning design can make a significant difference in our results. Workshops, although much maligned, can efficiently introduce staff to foundational knowledge and underlying theory. Workshops can also provide demonstrations of new skills in practice. Unfortunately, professional learning research has found that knowledge and demonstrations alone are not a sufficient platform for most educators to take the next steps, which involve transforming that information into new and consistent classroom practice.

This section will introduce the idea of weaving together multiple learning designs that assist teachers to move from learning about a new practice to supporting its use in the classroom. A single design is typically not sufficient to support teachers in this journey from awareness through implementation.

The learning designs standard focuses on three major concepts:

1. The selection and use of learning designs is based on learning theories, research, and models. These theories and research create a decision-making framework we use when making key decisions about learning designs.

   - For example, do we believe that adults need only to learn about new instructional theories and then they will be ready to implement those strategies in their classrooms? *If we don't, then a workshop is not a sufficient strategy to accomplish high-quality use of new practices. We will have to plan for demonstration lessons, collaborative planning, instructional coaching, and other support strategies.*

- Do we believe that all adults will learn at the same rate? *If we don't, we need to design a monitoring system that helps us determine what practices educators are using and provide differentiated support designs for individual or subgroups of teachers.*

- Do we believe that planning is a necessary element most educators require before they begin using new instructional strategies in the classroom? *If we do, then we need to build a schedule that provides time for Professional Learning Communities (PLCs) or grade-level teams to work together to create lessons and assessments and to teach those lessons, discuss their experiences, and refine lessons.*

Learning theories, research, and models inform us about how adults learn and how and when to use a variety of designs. These theories and research help us bring our underlying assumptions to the surface so we can examine them and—if need be—alter them.

2. The selection and use of a variety of learning designs is based on the desired results for educators and their students plus solid planning.

- Adults have preferred ways of learning, as illustrated by the beginning section of this volume provided by Ellie Drago-Severson. *We need to determine how our educators prefer to learn and what they believe is effective help and support.*

- An essential part of this element involves ongoing assessment, feedback, and coaching, so there is a high-quality implementation of new practices in the classroom. *How can colleagues provide feedback and peer coaching to each other to support implementation?*

- If PLCs are used, how do we help team members learn about a variety of learning designs, and how can we teach them to select appropriate learning designs that match their team's learning goals?

3. The most effective learning designs involve elements of active engagement. Active engagement structures learning, so colleagues interact with each other and the content during the learning process.

- Many protocols designed by the Annenberg Foundation use active engagement. For example, *The Four A's* protocol asks each participant to read an article or other selection and record (1) underlying **A**ssumptions, (2) ideas you **A**gree with, (3) ideas you would **A**rgue with, and (4) ideas you would **A**spire to **A**pply. These reflections are shared among members of a small group. Educators are, therefore, involved with reading, reflecting, and recording their responses to the reading, and sharing their thoughts in a small group.
- Lesson Study is a professional learning model that grew out of work in mathematics but has been applied to other content areas. It involves seven steps, which include teachers identifying an area of student need, jointly planning a lesson, one person implementing the lesson while others observe, a debriefing, and a revision of the lesson. Their engagement with each other through the process leads to better understanding of new strategies and higher trust among group members.
- In the Implementation volume of this series, Michael Fullan proposes that a collaborative school culture that emphasizes the quality and quantity of interactions and relationships among educators (or social capital) will have a much more successful implementation of new strategies and skills. He reports on a study that found teachers with lower skills who worked in a school with high social capital got better results than those who did not work in those kinds of environments. The interactions between and among educators result in educators learning from each other to improve instructional effectiveness. It is for this reason that many of the learning designs included in this chapter involve collaboration and interaction among colleagues.

Each of these three key elements will be described in more depth in the next section.

PLEASE PRESS YOUR PAUSE BUTTON

Double Clicking: Reflect on your current practices related to learning designs.

1. How does our current planning process match professional learning goals with our student learning goals?

2. In my school, what are the ways we involve teacher leaders and other staff members when making decisions about the professional learning designs we use?

3. How many different learning designs are currently used during school-wide and team-based learning (e.g., workshops, protocols, peer observation, co-teaching, examining student work)?

4. How does our school's or team's professional learning include support for classroom implementation of new strategies and practices?

APPLY LEARNING THEORIES, RESEARCH, AND MODELS

There's nothing more practical than a good theory.

Kurt Lewin

Learning theories, research, and models describe what is known about how adults learn. In some cases, the work specifically focuses on how educators learn. These theories, research, and models also create a decision-making framework we need to use when making key decisions about professional learning designs. Next, we'll examine a variety of studies that consider how adults and, sometimes more specifically, how educators learn and explain some of the implications.

State of Professional Learning in the Learning Profession (Darling-Hammond, Wei, Andree, Richardson, & Orphanos, 2009)

One of the purposes of current professional learning research is to determine whether or not educator professional learning impacts student outcomes. The reason for examining first whether professional learning impacts teacher and classroom practices is that there is little chance student learning will improve unless teachers' practices are enhanced or improved first. This relationship between adult learning and student impact is a fundamental belief of Learning Forward (formerly known as National Staff Development Council [NSDC], a national organization devoted to effective professional learning).

In 2009, an international study of professional learning, supported by Learning Forward, was published. This work described the characteristics, conditions, and types of professional learning processes that lead to changes in teacher knowledge, skills, and classroom practice, which, in turn, result in improved student learning. The findings are as follows:

1. Authentic and pervasive educator collaboration is necessary *spreads widely* for effective classroom use of new instructional, curricular, and behavioral practices. This finding corroborates Fullan's findings that collaborative cultures, where educators deprivatize their classroom lessons, strategies, practices, assessments, and outcomes and share ideas with each other improves all teachers' practices. The collaborative interactions between and among educators result in educators learning from each other about how to improve instructional effectiveness.

    Implication: Building strong collaborative relationships and school culture among educators at grade level, in content areas, and within the school supports and enhances instructional and curricular improvement. Collaborative relationships transcend congenial relationships where people are civil, respectful, and kind to each other. Those behaviors are the foundation of collaboration.

    Collaboration includes sharing ideas, resources, materials, and lessons; trusting colleagues enough to ask for help; engaging in problem-solving; sharing successes and failures; being open to other's ideas; providing feedback; and reflecting with others on the work. Many educators have said that their only interaction with colleagues occurs at the coffee pot, mailbox, or lunchroom. There is little time within the day to talk about challenges, share ideas, or ask about new resources. This reality has led some to view teaching as private practice. Collaboration calls educators to open up their classrooms and their teaching and to work with their colleagues—to deprivatize their practice. This is not merely an individual teacher issue but an organizational one as well. The organization assists in supporting collaboration by creating time for colleagues to meet within the day to discuss, plan, and learn together.

2. Impact on student learning requires deliberate, long-term support that assists educators in accomplishing high-quality implementation of new practices. The study's findings include that sustained and intensive professional learning for teachers is related to student achievement gains. What does this mean in practical terms? Intensive professional learning equals an average of 49 hours in a year. When this threshold is reached, it boosted student achievement by approximately 21 percent. This intensive work included building background content knowledge, demonstrations, practice and planning lessons, co-teaching with a coach or colleague, receiving feedback on the use of practice, and revising or amending strategies. It also can involve monitoring student work throughout the process to determine whether new strategies are making a difference in student learning.

   Implication: The most effective professional learning supports teachers from beginning awareness of an innovation or program through skill development and continues through job-embedded support, in order to ensure teachers use new practices within the classroom with quality. If you "launch 'em and leave 'em" (Kanter, n.d.) the innovation will only be used by a few trailblazers within the system and not have a significant impact for most students.

   Many principals can repeat the mantra that follow-up is necessary for effective professional learning but when pressed can't really give an example. Some of the tasks that need to be accomplished after beginning awareness and understanding have been developed include the following:

   • *Clearly define new practice in operation.* What are the critical attributes (Marzano, Pickering, & Pollock, 2001) of the new practices or essential components? What components are nice but not essential? Is there a clear picture of the new practice in operation? Critical attributes are essential characteristics of an instructional strategy. For example, the critical attributes for cooperative learning are (1) positive interdependence, (2) individual accountability, (3) face-to-face mutually beneficial interaction, (4) development of collaborative skills, and (5) process or debriefing (Marzano, Pickering, & Pollock, 2001). These components need to be in place before any small group can be considered a cooperative learning group.

The critical attributes of new strategies and models, or essential elements, need to be identified, reviewed, repeated, and accompanied by demonstrations or video examples until they are obvious and apparent to practitioners. (An Innovation Configuration map accomplishes this task; it is explained in depth in the Implementation volume of this series.)

- *Clarify misconceptions.* Despite our best efforts, adults walk away from good training with misconceptions about the new practice. For example, I found many educators believed that creating cooperative learning groups by counting off in Japanese (or some other interesting way) was a critical attribute. In fact, we consistently modeled interesting techniques during trainings, so it should not have been a surprise that this was misconstrued. Misconceptions reveal themselves as educators work with each other on learning tasks, planning, and observing classrooms.

- *Reinforce critical attributes (review using a new learning modality).* We might introduce critical attributes by giving a lecture accompanied by a video. The follow-up challenge is to create learning experiences that use different modalities—provide a video of a new strategy and engage small groups in labeling each critical attribute, or develop a written example of a lesson and cut it into components and ask staff members to reconstruct the lesson. You might ask small groups to create a metaphor for each critical attribute or make a poster that they could hang in their rooms, which reminds them of each essential part. This strategy also allows for differentiation by employing multiple intelligences within professional learning.

- *Plan for the use of new curriculum or strategies (with feedback).* According to Bruce Joyce and Emily Calhoun (2010) we are more likely to achieve successful implementation, especially of new curriculum, when we provide time for teachers to plan lessons, gather materials, and prepare for implementation. They found that educators are more likely to use new curriculum when they have had time to develop skills in planning lessons. These skills need to be at their fingertips and deeply understood, so they can use them with ease when planning courses and units of study, as well as individual lessons.

  Central office administrators in Kentucky upped the ante by also reviewing and providing feedback to planning teams early in the process of adopting Common Core curriculum in their districts; this review provided needed refinements to lessons and also allowed central office staff to diagnose misconceptions (Learning Forward, n.d.).

- *Problem-solving.* When implementation begins, there will be problems of practice that educators might not have encountered before. It might be as simple as a quick way to distribute manipulatives to small student groups or larger issues of students' reaction to inquiry lessons. These problems—large and small—can stop implementation of new practices. There are problem solving protocols which PLCs or other small groups can use to address these challenges and generate a list of possible solutions. (See Appendix A for Problem Solving Protocol).

- *Coaching (monitor and give feedback).* Coaching strategies can be conducted by an instructional coach or a knowledgeable peer. The power of coaching lies within a common understanding of the critical attributes—the person being observed as well as the coach need to know the attributes or components that are being looked for during the lesson. There should be no surprises. A second skill also required is the ability to give constructive feedback. Constructive feedback helps the observed teacher be open to learning and making revisions to practice rather than feeling evaluated (Armstrong, 2012).

- *Celebrate progress.* Celebrations always seem to occur at the end of a project. Celebrations also need to occur in-process, in order to acknowledge that educators and the organization are making progress, to signal that the organization has accomplished one of its intermediate benchmarks, and to recognize staff's efforts in making a change with the intention of impacting student learning. In an elementary school in Arizona, we stopped and celebrated their progress in improving reading achievement in the building. A decorated cake and sparkling apple cider were brought in during a staff meeting while the principal thanked staff members for their efforts towards meeting their school's goal of improved reading instruction. The cost was minimal—the impact on staff significant. (See Armstrong, 2013, for more on celebration.)

Research on the Components of Effective Training (Joyce & Calhoun, 2010; Joyce & Showers, 2002)

Bruce Joyce and Emily Calhoun's research on effective training (2010) identifies four essential components of an effective training program—particularly for new curriculum and models of teaching (see Figure 2.1). They were able to determine through a meta-analysis the impact of these components on participants.

Let's delve into each component. The study of rationale includes understanding the purpose of the new strategies and curriculum, as well as understanding when to use or not use those strategies. For example, participants will need to understand the theoretical underpinnings of inquiry learning within science instruction. Theory helps educators understand the purpose or rationale for use of new strategies or curriculum. The critical purpose of theory is to help educators make decisions about the use of the curriculum or strategies, as well as understand appropriate or inappropriate use. It is a decision-making tool. Unfortunately, the presentation of theory has gotten a bad name in many professional learning settings, perhaps because it is not followed by the other three components identified by Joyce and Calhoun. A quick look at Figure 2.1 may help us see why: Providing the rationale alone has minimal impact on short-term use (5–10%) as well as long-term use (5–10%).

Demonstrations of the curriculum or strategies in practice are also critical. Joyce and Calhoun found that at least 10 demonstrations are needed, and, if the innovation is complex, up to 25 or 30

Figure 2.1   Joyce and Calhoun's Training Components

Training Element	Effects on Knowledge	Effects on Short-Term Use (% of Participants)	Effects on Long-Term Use (% of Participants)
Study of Rationale	Very Positive	5–10%	5–10%
Rationale *Plus* Demonstrations (10 or more)	Very Positive	5–20%	5–10%
Rationale *Plus* Demonstrations *Plus* Planning of Units and Lessons	Very Positive	80–90%	5–10%
All of the Above *Plus* Peer Coaching	Very Positive	90%+	90%+

Source: Joyce & Calhoun (2010), p. 79. Used with permission.

may be required. These can be demonstration lessons that take place in a classroom and are observed by small groups of teachers. They could be videotaped lessons accompanied by a review of critical attributes. They could be case studies written by practicing teachers and include instructional materials. They might also be lessons co-taught by PLC members and observed by the remainder of the PLC, followed by a debriefing and discussion of critical attributes. Again, a quick review of Figure 2.1 shows that even when demonstrations accompany theory/rationale, the impact on both short-term (5–20%) and long-term use (5–10%) is still relatively low.

The next element that folds into the training model is planning. As mentioned in the preceding section, teachers need time to plan new lessons and units, gather materials, and prepare themselves for implementation. Joyce and Calhoun found this element to be the "key to implementation" (p. 77). Teachers need to be ready to go into their classrooms with already prepared strong lessons and accompanying student materials. In other words, they need time not only to prepare lessons and materials but to prepare themselves. In earlier work, Joyce and Showers found that practice of new strategies also needed to occur (2002). Literally, teachers practiced using the new strategies in a workshop setting where they would also receive feedback from instructors. They planned and conducted mini-lessons, where other participants acted as students. Again, a quick review of Figure 2.1 shows that when these three elements are employed together, there is a powerful impact on short-term use (80–90%) although not long-term use (5–10%).

The final component of training design is coaching. Initially, classroom coaching was conducted by outside specialists and expert trainers. Their coaching resulted in high levels of long-term use, but the costs were prohibitive. An alternative approach was tried—namely, using peer coaching teams who met together, shared ideas, and planned lessons that they all tried in their own classroom and analyzed after the fact. Discussing their own progress was an important element in these peer coaching groups. These peer coaching groups were able to support and sustain each other's use of innovations with over 90% of teachers using the new practices in the classroom.

Implication: When developing training programs, ensure that all four elements are included. In most cases, your school and district are already able to provide rationales and demonstrations. Ensuring there is time for small teams of teachers to plan together and receive feedback on their work and serve as peer coaches to each other will pay off in implementation of new programs. This element is an organizational responsibility, not an individual teacher one. I once had an administrator tell me that the basic information had been provided and now implementation was a responsibility of the teacher. This research on training argues against that assumption. If the organization espouses a new program, it also carries a responsibility to support teachers' use of that new program by providing time for planning, as well as for creating and supporting peer coaching teams.

Concerns-Based Adoption Model (CBAM) (Hord, Rutherford, Huling, & Hall, 2006, revised 2014)

The Concerns-Based Adoption Model, or CBAM, found that teachers move through a series of concerns as they learn about and use innovations (Hall & Hord, 2011). (Note that this research used teachers as subjects when developing the framework.) Those concerns can range from not being concerned at all about a new program to being ready to make adjustments to the new processes in order to revise and refine them. Each educator depending on his or her background and experience may react differently to the same innovation. The Stages of Concern model is presented in Figure 2.2.

Gene Hall and Shirley Hord also found that each of the concerns requires a different intervention to alleviate the concern and allow teachers to continue to move through the stages. Consider the flip side of that finding. Individuals will *not* automatically move through all seven stages; they can get stuck at a particular stage and not move past it—they suffer from arrested development!

For example, some teachers' concerns might match Stage 2: Personal concern. They are worried about how to find the time to learn the innovation and whether or not they can actually learn to use inquiry in science. They might have learned and been taught through lecture and recitation strategies and are not sure they can manage this new type of learning. If their personal concerns are not attended to and resolved, they might very well stall at this stage and never move beyond it—despite additional training, coaching sessions, and PLC work.

Figure 2.2   Stage of Concern

IMPACT	6	Refocusing	Considering alterations to the innovation
	5	Collaboration	Coordination and cooperation with colleagues
	4	Consequence	Impact of innovation on students
TASK	3	Management	Efficiency, organization, managing the innovation
SELF	2	Personal	Uncertain about the demands of using the innovation and his/her own adequacy in fulfilling those requirements
	1	Informational	General awareness and interest in learning more
	0	Unconcerned	Little awareness or concern

Source: From Figure 3.1: Stages of Concern: Typical Expressions of Concern About the Innovation in *Taking Charge of Change* (p. 31), by S. M. Hord, W. L. Rutherford, L. Huling, & G. E. Hall, 2006, revised 2014. Austin, TX: SEDL. Revised PDF version available from http://www.sedl.org/pubs/catalog/items/cha22.html. Reprinted by Corwin with permission from SEDL.

Fear not—there are recommended interventions for each stage. For example, for the personal concern stage,

- let the person know their concerns are legitimate,
- provide encouragement by pointing out individual skills and abilities related to the task,
- connect individuals with others who have moved beyond that stage and who can give counsel and support, and
- show how the innovation can be implemented in small steps instead of all-at-once (Hord, Rutherford, Huling, & Hall, 2004, p. 44).

Implications: There needs to be a monitoring system in place to diagnose and support individuals and small groups at the different stages of concern. There are easy and fast diagnostic strategies described in the Stages of Concern work that will be found in the Implementation standard volume of this series. Instructional coaches and PLC members can also learn about these stages to help them make decisions about their own professional learning strategies and needs.

As discussed in the first chapter of this book, one of the important issues to consider in professional learning is differentiation. CBAM provides another way to address differentiation through diagnosing and use of interventions focused on different stages of concern.

PLEASE PRESS YOUR PAUSE BUTTON

Double Clicking: Reflect on current professional learning designs.

Identify a high priority program your school or district has adopted and reflect on the components of effective professional learning using the following reflection questions. If you can, conduct this reflection in a small group, school leadership team, or district professional learning committee.

1. How do we use data to determine student learning needs and corresponding educator learning needs? Who conducts the data analysis? How are staff members involved in the analysis?

(Continued)

(Continued)

2. How well have we provided long-term assistance to staff members to support their use of innovations or new programs in their classrooms? (Is there concentrated time—for example, 49 hours in a single focus area?).

3. When we develop a training program, which of the essential components (rationale, demonstration, planning, and peer coaching) do we include? Are there any components we have not used?

4. How have we identified and communicated the critical attributes of new strategies to staff members and administrators?

5. How do we currently monitor implementation? How is that monitoring information used to differentiate support for teachers?

6. How have we created schedules to provide time for collaborative learning teams or PLCs to work together to plan lessons, solve problems, and support each other's use of new strategies?

Alone or with your small group, discuss the following questions:

1. What are the strengths of your current professional development?

2. What are the needs of your current professional development?

3. What next steps could/should you take to improve your current professional development?

4. What barriers exist that might block your next steps? What supports exist that might strengthen your next steps?

SELECT LEARNING DESIGNS

Not just anything called staff development will generate increased student learning. But some kinds of professional development can produce substantial gains—and in a relatively short period of time.

Bruce Joyce and Beverly Showers, 2002

Powerful professional learning results in application in the classroom.

Lois Brown Easton, 2008

Effective professional learning includes two goals: (1) changes in teacher practice, (which result in) (2) improved student learning. According to the research cited in the first section of this chapter, effective professional learning needs to accomplish multiple and layered outcomes:

- build the knowledge base, understanding, and rationale for new programs, strategies, or curriculum;
- develop skills to use new curriculum and/or instructional practices;
- support planning for and implementation of new practices; and
- engender the disposition required for high-quality implementation of new practices.

It will be difficult for a single professional learning design to accomplish all these outcomes. Rather than merely replacing the traditional workshop with an alternative learning design, professional learning planners need to think of a sequence of learning designs or strategies that will result in effective classroom use of new standards and instructional practices. Professional learning designers cannot be satisfied with merely building educator knowledge and skills, although that can be a gigantic task in itself. The goal of professional learning also should include strategies which support classroom implementation of new standards and practices. Implementation cannot be left to luck, hope, or chance. Planning of professional learning designs also needs to target strategies, designs, and activities that support and refine implementation.

The selection of professional learning designs begins with clear outcomes for student learning and identifying educator learning outcomes that correspond with that student learning goal. (A more detailed description of this process can be found in the Learning Communities volume in this series.) That learning outcome is the foundation. Improved student learning will not occur because a new and different design is used; it will more likely occur when the design aligns with the learning goal for educators. That outcome requires matching a wide array of learning designs to the needs of educators as they move from knowledge, to skills, to implementation. Professional learning becomes a tapestry, which contains multiple designs and strategies woven together into a coherent image. Let's look at an example of multiple designs in practice. We'll start with a relatively simple example and then move to a more complex one.

1. An elementary school identifies that they need to dramatically increase mathematics achievement across the grade levels. Teachers realize that they know how to teach students to use algorithms but need to go beyond procedural learning and create learning tasks that require students to devise strategies showing their understanding of mathematics concepts.

   The district mathematics specialist, working with the school coach, develops a workshop that focuses on this topic. It provides an explanation of the underlying rationale for the shift in instruction and also provides examples of lessons that develop student understanding of mathematics concepts. Teachers also participate in mathematics activities, which require that they devise their own methods for explaining their results. Many of these tasks are completed in small learning teams, and the lesson components are identified and labeled.

   The district specialist and school coach next provide demonstration lessons at each grade level and revise the schedule so appropriate grade-level instructors can observe the demonstration lessons. After each lesson, they hold a debriefing to point out key teacher actions.

   Grade-level PLCs use their weekly time to develop lessons for upcoming mathematics classes. The lessons are reviewed by the district specialist and school coach and feedback is provided to the teams. Sometimes, the lesson requires revisions. Each teacher teaches the lesson, and the group reflects on how they felt and also reviews student work.

   Teachers write statements describing their concerns when using the instructional strategies in the classroom. Small groups, across all grade levels, are formed for targeted learning sessions which address those concerns.

   Teachers decide to develop lessons independently and review them in their PLCs and provide feedback. The PLC assigned upcoming topics among group members so that everyone would benefit from the lessons. The school coach continues to monitor lesson development and occasionally works one-on-one with individual teachers.

2. A middle school analyzes their student achievement results from state and district benchmark assessments and decides staff need to focus on improving reading comprehension skills of informational text. They realize this is a focus for all content areas, not only the English faculty. They focus on instructional strategies and materials that increase reading comprehension of informational text.

The faculty begins with a book study that concentrates on informational text—recognizing that some content areas have specialized embedded vocabulary. PLCs conduct the book study using discussion protocols, and structured discussions are also held during staff meetings in cross-team groups to ensure there is a common understanding about their learning. Faculty also has opportunities to pose questions and challenge some of the information presented in the book. The district's reading instructional specialist monitors the book study so he can supply additional information and locate supplementary resources for the teams.

Interdisciplinary teams analyze their students' reading comprehension scores and identify specific areas of need. In short sessions on early release days, the district specialist introduces reading strategies and identifies critical attributes of those strategies. He engages the staff in a lesson that uses the strategies and asks them to reflect on how it was different or similar to strategies they already use. A series of videos are available for teams to view and identify the critical components. These videos demonstrate reading comprehension strategies in a variety of content areas. The reading specialist also provides demonstration lessons in content areas, and teachers' schedules are adjusted so that they can observe the demonstrations.

Teams from each content area have time weekly to plan lessons using these new reading strategies. The School Leadership Team, administrators, and district specialist review these plans and provide feedback to the teams. After some revision, team members commit to using the strategies in their classrooms and engaging in a reflection with their colleagues. This planning, practice, and debriefing activities are continued for 6 weeks.

The school's leadership team decides to determine the extent to which teachers are using the new instructional strategies and materials. As a team, they develop a list of key indicators based on the critical attributes and conduct walk-throughs of every classroom in the school. They also interview students and examine bulletin boards and samples of student work. They summarize the results and share their findings during a staff meeting. The staff uses this data to identify strategies that require additional focus and practice. They also identify barriers to using these new strategies. The teams create a schedule for peer observations and debriefings that focus on reading comprehension strategies. Based on results, the teams conduct an online search for content-based reading lessons plans that can be adapted for their classrooms.

PLEASE PRESS YOUR PAUSE BUTTON

Double Clicking: Analyze the examples of multiple designs.

1. What learning designs were used to build knowledge and develop rationales for new strategies?

2. What learning designs were used to build skills for the new strategies?

3. What learning designs were used to support implementation?

4. How did the learning designs contribute to collaborative interaction among faculty?

Multiple Learning Designs

Selecting an appropriate learning design is based on having a clear result in mind and an underlying theory about the sequence of learning that is most appropriate for your faculty members. A theory of change is suggested in this section, and it is derived from the work of Laura Desimone (2009). See Figure 2.3.

The transformation from gaining new knowledge about content standards and instructional practices to actually using them well within the classroom setting requires a sequence of learning. This sequence should be familiar with one difference: Desimone begins the sequence with ensuring that educators have the skills to work with each other in small and large learning teams. You'll see that

Figure 2.3   Theory of Change for Collaborative Professional Learning Teams

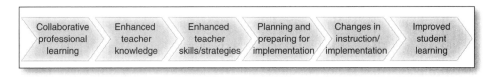

Source: Adapted from Desimone (2009).

skill is important because a majority of learning designs described in this section employ collaborative learning among PLCs or staff members. These collaborative skills cannot be assumed; teachers, until very recently, could do their job without much collaborative work with their colleagues. Making shared decisions, deprivatizing their practice, and problem-solving challenges to their work requires trust and risk-taking. This reality will be explained in more depth in the next section.

We begin the theory of change with building teacher knowledge about the content standards and appropriate instructional strategies. Next, learning designs are used to develop teacher skills and class-room practices related to their goals, explaining what they should do during instruction. The next phase involves lesson planning and preparation for implementation. This phase is necessary for strong implementation and is an organizational responsibility. Fourth, coaching and collegial assistance support teachers' use of new instructional practices and strategies in the classroom. Finally, when classroom instruction and curriculum have been transformed or modified to align with new curriculum standards, programs, or improvement goals, then data are collected to determine the impact on student learning. The reason student learning data are collected at this stage is that this forges the connection between changes in teacher practice resulting in student improvement. If a team or school or district cannot first demonstrate that teachers' practices have been amended, they cannot truly connect changes in student learning to anything teachers may or may not have done. The goal for the evaluation of professional learning is to correlate changes in teacher practice with improvement of student learning. Too many districts and schools assume their professional learning programs are working when student achievement improves; this assumption would be called into question from an evaluation perspective.

Unfortunately, most learning designs do not come with the same kind of labeling we might find on a can of soup. Designs won't indicate in their description whether it is useful in developing knowledge or skills or supports implementation. There are some designs that can be used within multiple phases of our theory of change. More research needs to be done that will help us tease out best use of these strategies. Until then, research and best practice will be the foundation for tables that will follow. These tables will define a variety of learning designs and also provide references where you can find more information about the learning designs. Next, using the phases of Theory of Change presented above, the best use of the learning designs will be indicated—are they useful for building knowledge, developing skills, planning and preparing for implementation, or supporting implementation?

Some of the learning designs are complete models of professional learning and include a series of strategies that traverse all the phases of the theory of change. Lesson Design is one of those models. Lois Brown Easton (2008) referred to these more comprehensive models as "container" designs that include multiple strategies. Container designs will be indicated in the tables by an asterisk.

Table 2.1 will provide a definition of the learning design and references where you will be able to find more detailed information to help you use this design.

ৡৼ

Table 2.2 (pages 74–77) provides more information about learning designs by designating a targeted purpose or use. You'll notice that most of the learning designs can be used for multiple purposes. A quick explanation of each of the descriptors follows:

Builds content or instructional knowledge. This is the first stage of the theory of change presented above. We usually think of this phase as beginning or awareness level; however, a number of change theories and models inform us that educators will continue to learn and seek more in-depth understanding of new curriculum or strategies as they use these new strategies, practices, and curriculum in their classroom. These designated learning designs could be used to build a foundation in a subject or assist educators in delving more deeply into the subject.

(Text continues on page 71)

Table 2.1

Learning Design	Description	References
3 Levels of Text	The purpose of this discussion protocol is for a small group to construct meaning collaboratively, expand thinking about, and clarify a specific text, podcast, videotape, article, or reading using increasingly specific descriptions. The structured protocol builds common understanding about new information both in small groups and within a whole group.	Richardson, J. (Feb./March 2009). 3 levels of text. *Tools for Schools.* National Staff Development Council, p. 5. www.learningforward.org
Action Research*	Action research is a process in which participants (teachers, principals, support staff, coaches) examine their own practice, systematically and carefully, using research techniques. It allows educators to explore topics related to their work and interests. The process is a learning experience as well as the results. Action research can be done alone or in a group.	Richardson, J. (Feb./March 2000). Teacher research leads to learning, action. *Tools for Schools.* National Staff Development Council. www.learningforward.org Caro-Bruce, C. (2008). Action research. In L. Easton, (Ed.), *Powerful designs* (pp. 63–70). Oxford, OH: National Staff Development Council.
Authors' Assumptions	This protocol helps educators delve deeper into a text by uncovering the author's underlying assumptions. This protocol results in a more informed interpretation of the text. This is useful with a text that primarily focuses on the author's opinion and can come from educational journals and magazines.	Killion, J., & Roy, P. (2009). *Becoming a learning school.* Oxford, OH: National Staff Development Council. Tool 11.11.

(Continued)

Table 2.1 (Continued)

Learning Design	Description	References
Case Discussion	Case Discussion learning design prompts a discussion of intricacies, ambiguities, and complexities of the classroom. Classroom life and interactions can originate from narratives or videos and illustrate common dilemmas and challenges that many educators will face. The discussion engages educators in careful reasoning of classroom situations and asks them to make reasoned judgments about how to handle the situation. Some of the outcomes that can be accomplished through Case Discussion include strengthening and extending subject content and pedagogical reasoning, uncovering underlying assumptions about instruction and opportunities to challenge one's own beliefs, generating and evaluating alternative teaching strategies; and analyzing student thinking.	Barnett-Clarke, C., & Ramirez, A. (2008.) Case discussions. In L. Easton (Ed.), *Powerful designs* (pp. 85–94). Oxford, OH: National Staff Development Council.
Classroom Walk-Throughs	Classroom walk-throughs are an informal, non-evaluative strategy for observing classrooms, which last only one to five minutes in each classroom. The data collected, by peers, administrators, instructional coaches, or specialists, are used to engender reflective dialogue among colleagues and administrators. Educator self-reflection and self-analysis are some of its intended outcomes. The walk-through process entails short classroom observations with reflective questions and conversations. The focus of the walk-through can include building a picture of teaching and learning used in the school, understanding what standards are being taught, examining student groupings or differentiation strategies, or identifying progress in the use of new strategies or curriculum. This learning design can serve multiple purposes depending on the observation focus.	Downey, C. (2008). Classroom walk-throughs. In L. Easton (Ed.), *Powerful designs* (pp. 95–106). Oxford, OH: National Staff Development Council.

Learning Design	Description	References
Coaching*	Supporting implementation of new practices is an essential component of effective professional learning. There must be active and intentional support for teachers as they learn to use new classroom practices. Classroom coaching provides differentiated professional learning support for educators. Coaching can include demonstration lessons with students, using current classroom materials. Co-planning and co-teaching lessons are conducted in the teacher's classroom. And finally, the teacher plans and the coach observes and gives feedback. The purpose of this sequence is to build teacher skill and proficiency in using new strategies.	Killion, J., Harrison, C., Bryan, C., & Clifton, H. (2012). *Coaching matters.* Oxford, OH: Learning Forward. Kise, J. (2008). Differentiated coaching. In L. Easton (Ed.), *Powerful designs* (pp. 143–154). Oxford, OH: National Staff Development Council.
Collaborative Assessment Conference	Created by Project Zero, this protocol focuses on a team of teachers examining student work, describing, asking questions, and exploring implications for instruction. An experienced facilitator is needed for this process. There is a presenting teacher who provides the student work and a series of steps taken to analyze the work and what the student might have been focusing on. Time to identify implications for instruction and an opportunity for participants to think about the process of their own thinking also occur during the protocol.	Killion, J., & Roy, P. (2009). *Becoming a learning school.* Oxford, OH: National Staff Development Council Tool 11.7.
Common Assessment Planning	In this learning design, educators from the same grade level work collaboratively to develop assessments that focus on new standards at the appropriate level of understanding. By developing, administering, and scoring common assessments, teachers can learn a great deal—how to calibrate their expectations against those of other teachers teaching the same grade or course. They learn how other teachers assess student learning and can compare it to their own practices. They learn what aspects of a concept other teachers stress. Common assessments are tools that teachers develop together to assess student learning. Teachers use common assessments to ensure they have common expectations about student work and that there is consistency in student learning. Teachers in cross-grade-level or course teams can develop common assessments to use frequently or periodically throughout the school year.	Killion, J., & Roy, P. (2009). *Becoming a learning school.* Oxford, OH: National Staff Development Council Tool 11.2.

(Continued)

Table 2.1 (Continued)

Learning Design	Description	References
Co-Teaching	Co-teaching and collaboration is a model that pairs a general education teacher with specialists to co-plan and co-teach lessons. For example, this might involve an ESL (English as a Second Language) specialist to work in a general education classroom to model how to enhance an ELL (English Language Learner) student's oral and literacy skills during Reading and Writing Workshop time. It can involve a variety of alternative models such as a single group of students with both teachers taking turns providing instruction, or students divided into two separate groups and learning the same content while the two teachers use different strategies.	Honigsfeld, A., & Dove, M. (March 2010). From isolation to partnership. *Teachers Teaching Teachers* 5(6), 1–4. www.learningforward.org
Critical Friends Groups*	Critical Friends Groups (CFGs), developed by the National School Reform Faculty, study their own teaching practices, build a shared knowledge base, and talk in-depth about student work, teacher tasks, and professional dilemmas. CFGs are based on a simple foundation—a structured professional conversation which provides colleagues time to learn with and from each other about their work. A CFG is comprised of 6–10 colleagues who meet monthly for at least 2 hours. Protocols—structured and timed frameworks—are used to guide the conversations and ensure members stay focused, ensure that everyone has a chance to talk, and ensure a mixture of sharing, reflection, questioning, and summarizing. Protocols create a safe environment for colleagues to discuss and improve instruction.	Quate, S. (2008). Critical friends groups. In L. Easton (Ed.), *Powerful designs* (pp. 107–114). Oxford, OH: National Staff Development Council.

Learning Design	Description	References
Curriculum Design	Designing curriculum means defining and organizing what is taught to improve student learning. To design curriculum, educators must identify what should be learned and taught. Educators also need to sequence the curriculum, determine which instructional techniques are appropriate, and decide when and how to assess learning. The process begins with examining student learning standards, constructing a curriculum map, organizing the curriculum to identify logical connections, and designing units of study and weekly plans. Materials and resources, as well as daily lessons and activities, complete the cycle. This sequence is especially important when new learning standards are introduced and alignment between those standards and daily instruction is needed.	Fitzharris, L. H. (2008). Curriculum design. In L. Easton (Ed.), *Powerful designs* (pp. 115–122). Oxford, OH: National Staff Development Council.
Descriptive Review protocol	When a teacher has questions about a specific student's learning, a descriptive review is a useful tool. It focuses on a detailed description of a student and his/her work. This protocol requires an experienced facilitator. Participants are asked to look for values, principles, and habits of mind. They describe what they see in the work, and overall critical themes and patterns are summarized. Participants offer recommendations to the presenting teacher. The presenting teacher shares any new insights into the child or the work.	Richardson, J. (Feb./March 2001). Descriptive review. *Tools for Schools* 4(4), 6. www.learningforward.org
Lesson Study*	Tests and student work help educators understand what to improve; lesson study helps teachers understand *how* to improve. It is an improvement structure that originated in Japan and focuses on what teachers want students to learn based on data analysis and schoolwide goals. In lesson study, a group of teachers develop a lesson together; one of them teaches it while group members observe student learning. The group discusses the lesson and often revises and re-teaches the lesson based on their analysis. This can develop a	Richardson, J. (Feb./March 2004). Lesson study: Teachers learn how to improve instruction. *Tools for Schools*. Oxford, OH: National Staff Development Council. www.learningforward.org

(Continued)

Table 2.1 (Continued)

Learning Design	Description	References
	professional learning culture where educators feel comfortable sharing with and observing each other. The focus is the lesson, not the individual teacher.	Lewis, C. (2008). Lesson study. In L. Easton (Ed.), *Powerful designs* (pp.171–184). Oxford, OH: National Staff Development Council.
Looking at Student Work	Examining student work provides educators with a unique portal into the classroom. It can help teachers better understand what individual students or groups of students have learned or not learned. It can uncover misconceptions as well as learning strengths. Examining student work also helps a team of teachers calibrate their expectations for student learning for greater consistency from classroom to classroom. Educators can learn a tremendous amount by looking at a teacher's assignment and the student work related to that assignment. The process typically involves teachers bringing one or more samples of student work for the group to analyze and discuss. There are many protocols that can be used to structure the conversation and ensure the conversation stays thoughtful and respectful rather than evaluative.	Richardson, J. (Feb./March 2001). Group wise: Strategies for examining student work together. *Tools for Schools 4*(4), 1–7.
Peeling a Standard	This learning design helps teachers make instructional and assessment decisions by examining the Common Core or other student standards, as well as the cumulative progress indicators above and below their grade level. Teams of teachers begin by examining and identifying the essential learning (content and skills) within the student learning standards, as well as the cumulative progress indicators for each strand for the grade levels below and above their current grade level. When teachers know what students are expected to know and should be able to do in order to demonstrate mastery in terms of cumulative progress indicators, they can focus instruction and assessment on essential learning and appropriate levels of understanding.	Killion, J., & Roy, P. (2009). *Becoming a learning school.* Oxford, OH: National Staff Development Council Tool 11.1

Learning Design	Description	References
	Within each content area, the team identifies a specific standard and develops a descriptive statement of the (a) focus, (b) content, and (c) levels of student understanding. For each strand within that standard, they also identify the progress indicators for the grade level below and the grade level above their grade level. They also identify the content and skills identified within the strands for their own grade level.	
Peer Observation/ Coaching	Peer coaching is an opportunity for teachers to observe each other during classroom instruction. Some reasons that teachers may want to engage in peer observation is to (a) see a new teaching strategy in action, (b) learn a new model of instruction, or (c) analyze classroom processes and procedures such as classroom management. This is one of the most authentic strategies of differentiated, job-embedded professional learning. It is more than a casual visit to a colleague's classroom; it needs to involve a specific purpose for the observation, norms during observation, debriefing, and observer reflection.	Lock, K. (October, 2006). Dear colleague, please come for a visit. *Teachers Teaching Teachers 1*(2), 1–5.
Planning Lessons Collaboratively	Planning lessons collaboratively in PLCs, grade-level teams, or content-focused teams uses the power of the group to prepare to put new strategies or curriculum into practice. Preparatory work includes knowledge of new curriculum or instructional strategies. Critical attributes for new strategies should be shared and understood so that the lesson can be reviewed with those standards in mind and appropriate feedback provided before use. Feedback could be provided by administrators, specialists, or colleagues. Planning has been recognized as critical to implementation. Locally developed planning frames and student standards are helpful.	

(Continued)

Table 2.1 (Continued)

Learning Design	Description	References
Say Something Protocol	This protocol is useful when participants are asked to read a specific text and make meaning from it during a staff or learning team meeting. The article, text, or reading is divided into meaningful segments. Pairs are formed. Each person reads silently until they reach the end of the segment. Then, each answers one of the provided questions. The whole group has a discussion about the selection when everyone has finished reading.	National School Reform Faculty www.nsrfharmony.org/protocols.html
Standards in Practice*	Developed by the Education Trust, this process serves as a quality control tool for analyzing and improving the quality of instruction. The process involves a close examination of teachers' assignments, student work, and the relevant standard or set of standards. This process is usually facilitated by a coach. A classroom assignment is described and participants complete the task. They align the content with national standards and create a scoring rubric. They use the rubric to score student work. The presenting teacher summarizes what has been learned and identifies next steps.	Mitchell, R. (1999, Summer). Examining student work. *Journal of Staff Development 20*(3), 32–33. www.learningforward.org Mitchell, R., & Kennedy-Salchow, S. (2008). Standards in practice. In L. Easton (Ed.), *Powerful designs* (pp. 229–241). Oxford, OH: National Staff Development Council.
Success Analysis Protocol	The purpose of this protocol is to identify the successful elements of an assignment, lesson, assessment, meeting, workshop, or collaborative group process. Emphasizing the positive aspects of educators' work is important especially when their work is in the midst of change. Groups include 3–8 members. A timekeeper and facilitator are needed for this protocol so that it moves quickly and crisply. A time-saving step is to ask each member to write his/her story of success beforehand and bring it to the team meeting. Group members discuss what they heard and the presenter summarizes what they heard, insights, and what they learned from the process.	National School Reform Faculty www.nsrfharmony.org/protocols.html

Learning Design	Description	References
Teacher Rounds*	Small teams of teachers engage in solving a shared, compelling problem of practice by observing and debriefing each other's classroom lessons. The purpose is to improve student learning while building a collaborative professional culture and collective responsibility. The process involves (1) Identifying a problem of practice, (2) Observing a classroom lesson, (3) Debriefing the lesson using a protocol, and (4) Making a commitment to experiment with new practices in each classroom related to the common problem of practice. This experiment is documented in a Record of Practice, which is shared with members of the team. The rounds follow a monthly cycle. A trained facilitator is needed and each member is required to attend a preparation and induction workshop to prepare them to participate in the work.	Troen, V., & Boles, K., with Pinnolis, J., & Scheur, A. (2014). *The power of teacher rounds.* Thousand Oaks, CA: Corwin Press.
Tuning Protocol	The Tuning Protocol, developed by the Coalition of Essential Schools, was originally designed to provide teachers with feedback on authentic assessments of student work. It can also be used to provide feedback on school- or team-based professional learning plans. One person serves as a presenter and also develops a focusing question related to the materials being reviewed. It is helpful to designate a facilitator who keeps track of time and ensures the feedback aligns with the focusing question. The presenter asks a focusing question that participants answer. Individual writing, participant discussion, and presenter reflection also occur within the protocol.	Easton. L. (Feb./March 2001). Tuning protocol. *Tools for Schools, 7*(3), 3. www.learningforward.org Easton, L. (2008). Tuning protocols. In L. Easton (Ed.), *Powerful designs* (pp. 265–272). Oxford, OH: National Staff Development Council.

(Continued)

Table 2.1 (Continued)

Learning Design	Description	References
Video-enhanced Professional Development* (VPD)	Video-enhanced Professional Development (VPD) promotes the use of classroom videos to improve and refine instruction. The process includes videoing teacher and student classroom behaviors, using the video to identify student and adult learning goals, using the video to collect teacher and student data, and engaging in a dialogue between the teacher and outside observers to refine practice and impact student learning, behaviors, or attitudes. VPD can be used by the teacher individually to support an individual professional growth plan, between a teacher and coach, among teams of teachers, and between a teacher and an administrator. Research has found that viewing a video of one's teaching can encourage change by helping educators, coaches, and administrators get a clear picture of what it looks like when they do their work and how students respond to instruction.	Knight, J. (2014). *Focus on teaching: Using video for high impact instruction.* Thousand Oaks, CA: Corwin Press.
Wagon Wheel	A Wagon Wheel protocol creates opportunities for colleagues to have four conversations with different people using discussion prompts about a selected text or common information and to brainstorm ideas for further action. This protocol also builds communication and connections between participants.	Easton, L. (Feb./March 2009). Protocols: A facilitator's best friend. *Tools for Schools 12(3)*, 4.

*Model or container learning design—involves multiple strategies

Reinforces knowledge of critical attributes. Knowing the critical or essential components of a new strategy is important because it helps us make decisions about what is nice but not necessary when we are beginning to use new practices. A single introduction of critical attributes is not sufficient; every video, demonstration, or case study needs to review and reinforce these attributes until they become part of the repertoire of educators. The critical attributes also serve as the foundation for defining the new practice in operation.

Develops skills. Change theory explains that there is a difference between "knowing" information about a new strategy and actually being able to perform that new strategy. It is called the knowing-doing gap. Skills here refer to behaviors that are used to plan and conduct instruction. I might be able to explain what dialogue is, but I also need actual language, phrases, and expressions when I participate in a dialogue.

Supports planning. Joyce and Calhoun found that deliberate and specific planning is the gateway to implementation. Collaborative lesson planning is an effective way to begin this phase. As grade-level or content-area teams plan together, they also clarify the big ideas, help colleagues transfer knowledge into practice, and reinforce critical attributes. Review and feedback on these initial plans is also beneficial because it reinforces understanding, refines skills, and serves as a monitoring system for coaches, central office and school administrators, and school leadership teams.

Supports implementation. Even though we might know what to do, we still might not actually use new practices during instruction. Sometimes implementation does not occur because sufficient planning has not taken place or materials have not been collected. Some adults may need many demonstrations and examples before they are ready to use new strategies with students. These learning designs support educators to take the step and use new materials and strategies in the classroom.

Particularly helpful in creating a learning community. Collaboration is a powerful cultural force in schools. Educators' learning from and with each other is a powerful form of professional learning and should be structured and reinforced during learning designs. Isolation does not lead to improvement; collaboration can ignite energy, commitment, and development of new skills and practices.

Focuses on standards, curriculum, and assessments. These learning designs specifically increase the understanding and use of new standards, curriculum, and assessment strategies.

Focuses on pedagogy and teaching. These learning designs focus on pedagogy and teaching. Many of them accomplish that task while examining student work to cement the relationship between instruction and learning.

Is particularly reflective. Reflection is an important component of many of the learning designs. Reflection on practice has been shown to be a powerful strategy, and it seems there is little time in many educators' days for such thoughtful reflection. Learning designs that use reflection as a major component of the design are included in this category.

Is helpful in problem solving. Challenges and concerns, similar to those mentioned in the Stage of Concern research, can literally stop educators from making progress in their use of innovation or new programs. Problem-solving strategies need to be built into professional learning to support educators as they move from beginning to expert use of new practices.

Results in a concrete product. Some of the learning designs develop specific products. This might be important information for summative or formative evaluation of professional learning. These products can be mined to assess how well staff members have learned new materials and practices or to determine whether they have attained intermediate benchmarks.

Is job-embedded. The term job-embedded needs explanation. There seems to be much confusion about the critical attributes of this concept. According to research, "Job-embedded professional development (JEPD) refers to teacher learning that is grounded in day-to-day teaching practice and is designed to enhance teachers' content-specific instructional practices with the intent of improving student learning. It is primarily school- or classroom-based and is integrated into the workday, consisting of teachers assessing and finding solutions for authentic and immediate problems of practice as part of a cycle of continuous improvement. JEPD is a shared, ongoing process that is locally rooted and makes a direct connection between learning and application in daily practice, thereby requiring active teacher involvement in cooperative, inquiry-based work" (Croft, Coggshall, Dolan, Powers, with Killion, 2010, p. 2).

Involves looking at student work or students. Student work not only helps educators understand individual students but also serves as a portal into analyzing instruction, assignments, and assessment. It is the authentic work of the classroom and a powerful professional learning tool. Student work grounds our professional conversation in the real world of work and student learning.

Table 2.2 is by no means the definitive list of learning designs. There are many others that school and district professional learning specialists develop every day that mirror learning strategies desired in classrooms. Table 2.2 represents a good mix of different types of strategies—some short protocols and others longer, job-embedded projects.

Using the Charts to Plan Multiple Professional Learning Designs

In reality, the sequential model of learning presented in Figure 2.3 rarely occurs so neatly in the real life of schools. Articles, research, and real life experience tell us progress is sometimes made more slowly than we expect, and our hypotheses about how quickly adults will learn and adopt new strategies and practices never quite seem to match reality. This is in part because there are multiple initiatives occurring within the same time and space for many teachers, and all those new practices are hard to juggle.

Figure 2.4 (page 78) might be a more realistic visual for the theory of change. Sometimes, we've completed our plans for providing background understanding and developing a new foundation, and our participants have not clamored for more information or are not asking questions, so we feel we can move on. A quick check might reveal that a majority of staff members are still not secure in the knowledge we hoped they would have gained. As with students, we must go back and reteach the material in a new way, using new learning designs and new modes of learning.

The process map in Figure 2.4 indicates that after each phase of the learning process, we should stop and check the progress of

(Text continues on page 79)

Table 2.2

Purpose and Characteristics of Professional Learning Designs

Professional learning designs	Builds content or instructional knowledge	Reinforces knowledge of critical attributes	Develops skills	Supports Planning	Supports implementation	Helpful in creating a learning community	Focuses on standards, curriculum, assessments
3 Levels of Text	X	X				X	
Action Research*	X		X		X	X	X
Author's Assumptions	X	X					
Case Discussion	X	X		X	X	X	X
Classroom Walk-Throughs		X					X
Coaching*	X	X	X	X	X		X
Collaborative Assessment Conference						X	
Common Assessment Planning		X	X	X	X	X	X
Co-Teaching	X	X	X	X	X		X
Critical Friends Groups*	X	X	X			X	X
Curriculum Design	X	X		X	X	X	X

Purpose and Characteristics of Professional Learning Designs

Professional learning designs	Builds content or instructional knowledge	Reinforces knowledge of critical attributes	Develops skills	Supports Planning	Supports implementation	Helpful in creating a learning community	Focuses on standards, curriculum, assessments
Descriptive Review Protocol						X	
Lesson Study*	X	X		X	X	X	X
Looking at Student Work		X				X	X
Peeling a Standard	X	X				X	X
Peer Observation/Coaching		X			X	X	
Planning Lessons Collaboratively		X	X	X	X	X	X
Say Something Protocol	X	X	X				
Standards in Practice*	X	X	X		X	X	X
Success Analysis Protocol					X	X	X
Teacher Rounds*	X	X	X	X	X	X	X
Tuning Protocol	X	X			X	X	
Video-enhanced Professional Development*		X	X	X	X	X	
Wagon Wheel	X	X				X	

(Continued)

Table 2.2 (Continued)

Professional learning designs		Purpose and Characteristics of Professional Learning Designs					
	Is particularly reflective	Helpful in problem solving	Results in a concrete product	Is job-embedded	Involves modeling	Involves looking at student work or students	Focuses on pedagogy and teaching
3 Levels of Text	X						
Action Research*	X	X	X	X		X	X
Author's Assumptions							
Case Discussion	X	X			X		X
Classroom Walk-Throughs	X			X			X
Coaching*	X	X			X	X	
Collaborative Assessment Conference	X	X	X			X	X
Common Assessment Planning			X	X		X	
Co-Teaching		X	X	X	X		X
Critical Friends Groups*	X	X	X			X	X
Curriculum Design			X	X			X
Descriptive Review protocol						X	

Purpose and Characteristics of Professional Learning Designs

Professional learning designs	Is particularly reflective	Helpful in problem solving	Results in a concrete product	Is job-embedded	Involves modeling	Involves looking at student work or students	Focuses on pedagogy and teaching
Lesson Study*	X	X	X	X	X	X	X
Looking at Student Work						X	
Peeling a Standard			X	X			
Peer Observation/ Coaching	X	X		X	X	X	X
Planning Instruction		X	X	X			X
Say Something Protocol							
Standards in Practice*	X	X	X	X		X	X
Success Analysis Protocol	X			X			
Teacher Rounds*	X	X	X	X	X	X	X
Tuning Protocol	X	X				X	X
Video-enhanced Professional Development*	X		X	X	X	X	X
Wagon Wheel							

*Model or container learning design—involves multiple strategies

Figure 2.4 Process Map—Multiple Professional Learning Designs

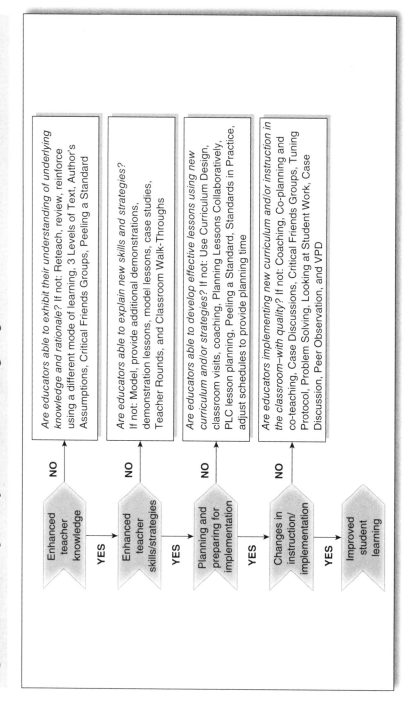

Enhanced teacher knowledge — NO → *Are educators able to exhibit their understanding of underlying knowledge and rationale?* If not: Reteach, review, reinforce using a different mode of learning, 3 Levels of Text, Author's Assumptions, Critical Friends Groups, Peeling a Standard

YES ↓

Enhanced teacher skills/strategies — NO → *Are educators able to explain new skills and strategies?* If not: Model, provide additional demonstrations, demonstration lessons, model lessons, case studies, Teacher Rounds, and Classroom Walk-Throughs

YES ↓

Planning and preparing for implementation — NO → *Are educators able to develop effective lessons using new curriculum and/or strategies?* If not: Use Curriculum Design, classroom visits, coaching, Planning Lessons Collaboratively, PLC lesson planning, Peeling a Standard, Standards in Practice, adjust schedules to provide planning time

YES ↓

Changes in instruction/implementation — NO → *Are educators implementing new curriculum and/or instruction in the classroom—with quality?* If not: Coaching, Co-planning and co-teaching, Case Discussions, Critical Friends Groups, Tuning Protocol, Problem Solving, Looking at Student Work, Case Discussion, Peer Observation, and VPD

YES ↓

Improved student learning

our educators. Did they learn what we wanted them to learn? Did they gain the skills that we focused on? Were they able to plan lessons using new curriculum and strategies? If the answer is no, then we need to return to, review, and reteach the appropriate content using a different method from that originally used. In the process map, the box which appears after the "No" refers to possible learning designs that are listed in the charts as well as other strategies that could be used.

The process map also serves as a reminder that professional learning plans should be designed with benchmarks when district, school, and teacher leadership pause to determine progress and make decisions about next steps. Some leaders from Kentucky districts reinforced this notion with me as they developed Innovation Configuration maps about how they rolled out development of Common Core standards (Learning Forward, n.d). These administrators laid out a detailed timeline but checked it each month to ensure they had actually accomplished their intermediate goals. They explained that they were overly ambitious concerning the amount of time this development would take. They had to go back and revise and redo some of their plans based on their monitoring of educators' lesson plans or outcomes.

Here is one way you might fit all of this information together into a plan for professional learning.

1. Based on your analysis of student learning data, benchmark assessments, and student work, identify a measurable student learning goal.

2. Working with staff, identify knowledge, classroom practices, and curriculum content knowledge educators need to know and be able to use in the classroom. Use this information to develop an educator professional learning goal. (For more detail about steps one and two, see the Learning Communities volume in this series.)

3. Develop your professional learning plan as usual. Stop and review the plans to see whether each of the phases of the Theory of Change (Figure 2.3) has been included in your plan. If each phase has not been planned for, refer to Figure 2.3 to add potential new learning designs.

Create intermediate benchmarks for professional learning. You might begin with using each phase, which serves as a natural benchmark and has a question built in (again, see the boxes to the right of the process map—Figure 2.4).

4. As you pause at each benchmark and assess educator progress and results, if more development work is required, again refer to the Figure 2.4 to identify potential learning designs. Remember Figure 2.4 also includes a reference that will provide more detailed information required for use of the learning strategy.

PROMOTE ACTIVE ENGAGEMENT

Tell Me, I Forget
Show Me, I Remember
Involve Me, I Understand

Chinese Proverb

The last essential element of the Learning Designs standard is ensuring that active engagement is a component of professional learning designs. This final element resonates with much of the current thinking about effective learning designs for our students. If they are involved rather than sitting and listening, they are more likely to learn and retain information. If they are engaged in discussion, dialogue, and application, they will be able to transfer their new learning to other settings and situations. If they are required to critique, create, and synthesize, they will develop a deeper and more critical understanding of the new learning. This is as true for adults as students.

All of the learning designs suggested in this chapter actively engage learners, and most also develop collaborative relationships among colleagues at the same time. The ultimate purpose is not to just build knowledge but also to build skills and support implementation. Professional learning is not just about bringing new information to staff and expecting or hoping for implementation. Professional learning also includes activities and conversations that support educators' use of new strategies in the classroom. This support is an organizational responsibility rather than an individual teacher responsibility (Joyce & Calhoun, 2010).

Following is one final example. Imagine that a school has identified a learning goal to improve student reading comprehension within the content areas. A learning team consisting of social studies teachers might begin by reading and discussing chapters of a book on reading strategies. They could use a discussion protocol to frame their conversation about the text. They could then begin to practice applying this information to the classroom by developing common lessons in their content area. Partners could draft lesson plans and request that other learning team members help them refine and improve the lesson through the use of another protocol such as the Tuning Protocol. After each pair's lesson has been reviewed and refined, the team could ask their instructional coach to review the lessons. Then, while the coach works with one classroom, the partners co-teach the lesson while other team members observe. Once the lesson has been completed, the partners plus other team members share their observations and revise the lesson again—if warranted. This process continues until members feel ready to write lessons independently and use them in the classroom. At this point, the members bring student work to the team meetings where they are analyzed to determine the impact on student learning. This team-based learning design includes active engagement, allows educators to select their own learning designs, and provides multiple opportunities for collegial collaboration.

CONCLUSION

Making decisions about learning designs involves more than understanding a wide array of potential designs. It involves diagnosing which phase of the learning process educators have reached. Are they at the beginning of learning about a new strategy or curriculum or are they in the throes of moving that knowledge into practice within the real context of students and multiple classroom demands?

Learning designs hold the allure, for some, that there is a *silver bullet* professional learning strategy that will resolve all the complicated issues involved in the process of change. Just as there is not a single instructional strategy that will meet the needs of all students, there is not a single professional learning strategy that will meet the needs of all adult learners. Educators, administrators, coaches, and professional learning professionals need to be able to diagnose educator progress against a theory of change, such as the one provided in this chapter, and determine whether staff members are ready to move forward or whether they need more time and emphasis on foundational knowledge and skills. This diagnosis will lead quickly to the need to differentiate professional learning because adult learners, similar to our students, will not learn in the same way nor at the same speed.

Collaborative professional learning, conducted within small school-based learning teams, requires that school staff, coaches, and administrators

- understand and adopt a theory of change based on current research and best practices,
- analyze data to determine a specific focus for adult learning based on student needs,
- clearly identify adult learning goals that include high-quality implementation of new practices,
- collect and understand a variety of professional learning designs,
- build the skills to diagnose which phase of the learning process educators are in,
- develop strategies and processes to differentiate learning and support for adult learners, and
- build skills and strategies that support educators to implement new strategies in their classrooms.

The primary outcome or result of effective professional learning design is the use of desired practices in most classrooms and schools. Without this kind of impact on educators, we will not be able to see the impact on student learning. That is why professional learning needs to be designed with implementation in mind—we owe it to our students to ensure they are getting the best education available.

REFERENCES

Armstrong, A. (2012, Summer). The art of feedback. *The Learning System, 7*(4), 1, 4–7.

Armstrong, A. (2013, Fall). Celebrate professional transitions and successes to drive and sustain implementation. *Tools for Learning Schools, 17*(1), 1–7.

Croft, A., Coggshall, J., Dolan, M., Powers, E., with Killion, J. (2010, April). Issue Brief: *Job-embedded professional development: What is it, who is responsible, and how to get it done well.* National Comprehensive Center for Teacher Quality, Mid-Atlantic Comprehensive Center, and National Staff Development Council. www.learningforward.org/docs/pdf/jobembeddedpdbrief.pdf?sfvrsn=O

Darling-Hammond, L., Wei, R. C., Andree, A., Richardson, N., & Orphanos, S. (2009, February). *Professional learning in the learning profession: A status report on teacher development in the United States and abroad.* Oxford, OH: National Staff Development Council and the School Redesign Network at Stanford University.

Desimone, L. (2009, April). Improving impact studies of teachers' professional development: Toward better conceptualizations and measures. *Educational Researcher, 38*(3), 181–199.

Easton, L. B. (2008). *Powerful designs for professional learning* (2nd ed.). Oxford, OH: National Staff Development Council.

Hall, G. E., & Hord, S. M. (2011). *Implementing change: Patterns, principles, and potholes* (3rd ed.). Upper Saddle River, NJ: Pearson.

Hord, S. M., Rutherford, W. L., Huling, L., & Hall, G. E. (2006, revised 2014). *Taking charge of change.* Austin, TX: Southwest Educational Development Laboratory (SEDL).

Joyce, B., & Calhoun, E. (2010). *Models of professional development: A celebration of educators.* Thousand Oaks, CA: Corwin Press and NSDC.

Joyce, B., & Showers, B. (2002). *Student achievement through staff development* (3rd ed.). White Plains, NY: Longman.

Kanter, R. M. (n.d.). *Are our change measures and milestones adequate?* www.reinventingeducation.org

Learning Forward. (n.d.). *Guiding District implementation of Common Core state standards: Innovation configuration maps.* www.learningforward.org/publications/implementing-common-core

Marzano, R., Pickering, D., & Pollock, J. (2001). *Classroom instruction that works: Research-based strategies for increasing student achievement.* Alexandria, VA: Association for Supervision and Curriculum Development.

APPENDIX A: PROBLEM SOLVING PROTOCOL

Step One: One person describes the problem s/he is having in great detail. Other people in the group listen and take notes.

Step Two: Other group members ask questions to get more information or to clarify aspects of the problem. The purpose is to understand the issue more fully (*Tell me about classroom demographics . . .*) rather than give advice (*Have you ever thought of . . .*).

Step Three: The group brainstorms possible solutions. Brainstorming can mean "off the wall" ideas; at this point, the group is looking for quantity, not quality. The person who presented the problem cannot speak because they are likely to say, "That won't work because . . . " which shuts down creative thinking and brainstorming.

Step Four: The group decides which solutions might work within the setting. They discuss pros and cons of each approach and identify the top five most practical solutions. The presenter is included in this discussion.

Step Five: The person who presented the problem now takes all the brainstorming ideas and rank orders the three to five ideas that might be used. This ranking allows the person multiple options for resolving the issue. They can start with the highest ranked idea, and if that doesn't solve the issue go on to try the next idea.

CHAPTER THREE

The Case Study

Valerie von Frank

USING THIS CASE STUDY

Most readers of this case study will find a district that is different from theirs. The temptation is to say this district is too rich or more disadvantaged, larger or smaller, more urban, more rural, more or less diverse. Doing so misses the value of a case study.

The questions at the heart of the matter are about how well this system stands up when we consider the major strands of this specific standard for professional learning. In reading the case study, it's fair to ask how the system meets the individual standard, as well as in what ways it may not. It's helpful to consider how well the district meets the other standards for professional learning, which top-performing systems generally do because of the interconnected nature of the standards. Most effective systems working to achieve one standard strive toward quality professional learning that meets multiple standards. But in the real world, as they reach, they also may fall short in one area or another.

The decision for this series to use real, journalistic-style rather than fictionalized case studies was deliberate. The intent is for readers to hear educators' voices from actual practice, to see examples of what is possible and what it looks like to work to the level of a specific standard for professional learning—including some aspects that may not fully exemplify the standard. The districts were chosen based on research, interviews, and solid evidence that student outcomes are improving, because student achievement is the ultimate goal of professional learning. Professional learning does not take place for its own sake, but to enable teachers to teach effectively so that every student achieves.

Often these days it seems we are tempted to focus on our differences rather than seeking the good we can find in the model before us. Reading a case study should invite that certain amount of critique, but also of recognition if not admiration. Rather than losing the point by focusing on differences and perceived shortcomings, we invite you to consider the standard at hand. Review its main components. Ask how this district exemplifies those elements. Listen carefully to what those at each level of the system said about learning from their vantage point.

Ask probing questions, either as a reader or with colleagues, and use the case as it is meant—for thoughtful discussion of a district's strengths, areas for improvement, and more than as a comparison with your own or an ideal, as a launching point for discussing how the standard for professional learning strengthens educators' core work and makes possible greater student achievement. When you have delved deeply into the standard itself, the next step is to look within your own district to determine how the standard can be used to improve your system.

At the end of the case study, you will find a set of discussion questions to prime your reflection, analysis, and discussion. We encourage you to meet and discuss this district's implementation of professional learning with a few colleagues and share your insights with other school and district staff.

The changes taking place in Hamblen County Department of Education are a snapshot of an altered nation. Tucked away in a corner of east Tennessee just a few stone skips from the Great Smoky Mountains National Park, this mid-sized, rural district has faced an evolving economy and a changing student demographic.

This is the region that gave birth to Davy Crockett and other fiercely independent frontiersmen. The Scots, Irish, and Germans who settled the area began as farmers until textile factories and furniture makers turned Morristown into a manufacturing hub in the 1930s. Those manufacturers yielded to a global economy less than a century later. Now, while manufacturing continues to employ nearly one in five—five times the national average—the companies employing people are mainly high-tech plastics manufacturers and automotive parts suppliers.

"It's almost like we are the Detroit of the south," said Brenda Dean, the school district's assistant director, "not in that [area industries] assemble cars, but we build every part of cars. We build seats, we build pistons, we build airplane parts, we build semi-truck parts, so there's a lot of advanced manufacturing." These companies have headquarters in Germany, Japan, Italy, among others, bringing what Dean calls "a lot of international influence into our little town," along with increasing pressure for an advanced workforce that can compete globally.

The changing economy and Great Recession have certainly shown their faces at the schoolhouse door. Where the number of students meeting federal poverty guidelines was 40% a decade ago, now the director of schools, the title given to what other districts call a superintendent, expects that rate to be closer to 70% in fall 2014. At the same time, the number of non-English speaking students taking a seat in these classrooms has exploded. About two of every 10 district students come to school needing to learn English, compared with just 1% only a decade ago—one child in an outlying school here or there within the district.

For Hamblen County educators, those changes have meant adjusting attitudes—attitudes toward teaching, toward testing, toward students.

LEARNING TO INCREASE RIGOR

Bradley Bays has taught for 14 years at Morristown West High School. The head of the social studies department said he started out teaching in the same ways he'd been taught. He expected students to arrive prepared, handed out homework, and penalized those who, for whatever reasons, didn't conform.

Bays said that after a half-dozen years of teaching, he began to recognize the student population was changing and that some students had greater opportunities in learning than others—those he jokingly referred to as "the pretty people." He learned that some of his students needed to work long hours after school to help at home or had to take care of family members, leaving less time to study. Bays began keeping paper and pencils on hand, and he began to adjust his grading, eliminating grades for homework.

"I simply had to switch my mindset," Bays said, "to make sure that we are allowing learning to be accessed by as many people as possible. I'm not going to penalize students grade-wise or not allow them some opportunities [because they didn't do homework] so that they get behind and then fail and quit."

Jeffrey Moorhouse, principal at Morristown West, said teaching and learning in the high school changed dramatically when the school began to rise to the challenge of increased state and district accountability.

With multiple pressures at play, the district joined the Southern Regional Education Board's (SREB) High Schools That Work, which focuses on improving instruction to raise student achievement. Teachers attended SREB conferences to share experiences and learn, and teachers districtwide focused on increasing rigor in student work and improving student engagement. Using grant funding, Morristown West began sending more teachers to Advanced Placement training.

"For example," Moorhouse said, "all of my regular biology teachers have gone to the same AP training as my AP biology teacher. So now they understand in biology what students are expected to know and do, and they can teach their regular biology course to that level of rigor. It's just being able to see what rigor looks like."

Moorhouse said the training not only is good for teachers' immediate learning but also offers them extended networking opportunities to continue to access resources, lessons, and advice.

Teachers' shared understanding of the level of rigor required to meet new standards built over time. Bays said that initially, some teachers looked at the instructional techniques in AP classes and said, "Well, I don't have those kids." Then another teacher would try some of the strategies and experience similar success. The practices spread slowly as teachers began to share within the department and even across the school, planned informally together, coordinated lessons and assessments, and looked at vertical alignment.

The school began offering freshmen the opportunity to take AP Human Geography. About a fourth of students now do so. Those who need just a bit more time to prepare for the most rigorous courses can take honors classes. Once students experience success in their freshman and sophomore AP or honors classes, Bays said, they are more ready and willing to tackle other rigorous college-preparatory courses using the reading and writing skills they've gained.

Within just 5 years, the number of AP classes offered to students at Morristown West increased from four to sixteen. The number of students taking AP classes in their junior and senior years continues to rise, all without a change in the proportion of students scoring a 3 or higher.

Bays said using AP approaches raised teachers' expectations for their practice: "We shared those same principles of 'Everyone can do it; let's look and see reasons that they can,'" Bays said.

Moorhouse said teachers' emphasis at the school has shifted from simply instructing to student learning.

"We have tried to take out students' excuse that 'I'm just not a good test taker' and give students multiple opportunities to meet the expectations," he said. "If you take the test and you're not at proficiency, then you go back and work on the standards that were not satisfactory. Once you've done some rework on those standards, then you can come back, show that to the teacher, retake the test, and improve the score—because ultimately it's about students knowing the material, not that they knew it by a certain deadline."

Hamblen County Department of Education comprises 11 elementary schools, 4 middle schools, 2 high schools, and an alternative school. Student enrollment is 10,208, of whom 74% are white, 16% Hispanic, 6% African American, and 4% Asian and other. In addition, 62% of students qualify for free or reduced-price lunch.

Overall, the county population is 10.9% Hispanic, twice the state average. Hamblen County has fewer college graduates and a lower per capita income than average for the state, and a slightly greater number of people live below the federal poverty level.

LEARNING FROM OTHERS

Some of the shift in attitudes began about the time the system hired a new head. Dale Lynch took the system's lead post as director of schools in 2001. Before long, he observed that the student population was changing. In meetings with lead administrators, he and other administrators began to ask themselves, "What are we going to do to make sure all students are learning at high levels?"

To find the answers, an administrative team visited districts facing similar challenges, traveling to Kentucky, Georgia, and Florida to understand what programs were working and what instructional practices were most effective. Then they spent more than a year planning what teachers would need to know and how they would learn to change their practices.

"When you talk about adult learning, it is very different than student learning," Lynch said. "The research is pretty clear on that."

The district first formed instructional leadership teams—school teams of three to five grade-level representatives who take their learning back to their buildings to teach colleagues. School-level instructional leadership teams explored Robert Marzano's research and began working with consultants Harvey Silver and Richard Strong on "thoughtful classrooms," a professional development approach that focuses on five questions:

- What skills do students need to develop in order to achieve at high levels?
- What instructional strategies enable the greatest gains in student performance?
- How can we address the diversity of our students in a way that is manageable and provides an equal opportunity for all students to achieve?
- How can we design units of instruction that motivate learners with different learning styles yet still address the skills and core content knowledge students need to succeed?
- How do schools become professional learning communities that support teachers through the improvement process?

Lynch said instructional leadership team members work directly with their colleagues on professional learning.

"Every teacher has their own growth plan and then they work with our instructional leadership team members to identify other programs or other opportunities out there for them to improve," the director of schools said. "And we've identified schools across our state, across our district that they can visit to learn new practices. It's like them having a tool box and just continuing to work with other schools in our district and across the state that will make them more effective."

LEARNING IN PROFESSIONAL LEARNING COMMUNITIES

The site-based instructional leadership team members translate their learning to other staff members within their buildings and work with grade-level learning teams. These teams have been essential to distributing learning throughout the district.

Team members look at student work samples and work with grade-level or subject area groups of teachers in learning communities at their buildings to identify struggling students, high-achievers, and those working at grade level in order to target students' specific needs. These lead teachers focus on increasing rigor, working with colleagues in learning communities to consider topics as specific as a criterion for how students learn to cite textual evidence or evaluating instruction that improves students' ability to compare and contrast.

"The teams have been very important whenever we make any instructional shift," Dean said. She said the collaborative efforts of teachers working together have moved the district forward.

"Implementing professional learning communities seemed to be the best hope of spreading strategies with some consistency," Dean said. "We knew that people needed support from colleagues—that there needed to be common learning if we were going to change outcomes for students. If I learn to work with my colleague and we share the best practices of both of us, then our learning doesn't have an additive effect—it's a multiplier. It's really about capacity building."

District leaders do not require schools to provide time for professional learning communities, according to Lynch, but schools try to provide common planning time. Morristown West math teacher Brian McLaughlin said administrators try to schedule teachers' planning periods to allow at least those teaching the same courses time to collaborate. McLaughlin said he worked with three colleagues last year on lesson planning and creating common assessments for key points in the curriculum.

"All of the teachers at some point or another gave me an idea that I could build on or [I gave them an idea that would] help them grow, and that was nice," McLaughlin said. "One challenge was that we weren't on the same page every day. One of us may teach the Pythagorean Theorem in November and the other one did it in February, so there's a fuzzy memory of what went well and what didn't." As a result, he said, teachers have made common pacing a goal.

"We're going to make sure our kids are going to end up in the same place overall," McLaughlin said.

Moorhouse, the Morristown West High School principal, said he and the assistant principals in his school each meet monthly with departmental learning communities, which also integrate other teaching specialty areas, such as agriculture science. They work to develop common quarterly assessments and focus on the standards students must meet.

For example, Moorhouse said, in the English department team he asked teachers to bring in samples of literature taught and the text-dependent questions teachers asked students, so the group could discuss the level of questioning and whether students needed to refer to the text in order to respond.

"Once we've given that quarterly exam," Moorhouse said, "we sit down and talk about which standards common across all of our classrooms are weak and we need to look at, or if there's one assessment or one standard that kids in one teacher's classroom missed compared to other teachers, then those teachers can have conversations."

"Professional learning communities aren't just a model for delivering new learning strategies," Rice said. "They are a model for teachers getting to evaluate student work to develop formative assessments, and we found that to be the best model as we come into new standards, into Common Core, into new [state] tests."

LEARNING FOR LEADERS

For the model to work, leaders also must be learners. District leaders insist that principals attend professional development with their instructional leadership teams, in order to know what to look for as changes are being implemented in instruction in the schools.

Principals then use informal, nonevaluative walk-throughs to look at the level of rigor in classrooms and how new strategies are being implemented. Walk-through teams use a rubric to give teachers a sense of how engaged students are, as well as the cognitive level of the tasks team members observed the teacher requiring of students. Principals have begun pairing up to co-observe teachers in one another's schools, providing valuable insights for the leaders about what teaching looks like in the district—and what to look for in exemplary instruction.

Principals not only attend professional development with their teachers, they also have targeted training in specific areas. For example, through the SREB, principals participated in units on building instructional leadership teams, analyzing student failure, and assessing academic rigor. Principals also have participated in book studies on their own, studying the work of Michael Schmoker, Daniel Coyle, James Stronge, Lucy Calkins, Jim Collins, and others. Their learning is focused on improving instruction.

Lynch holds principals accountable for teachers' growth as much as for student growth. Principals' evaluations include their communication with teachers and feedback they have provided on teacher lessons.

RELYING ON INTERNAL EXPERTISE

While much of school leaders' and teachers' learning is embedded, the district requires that teachers participate in 21 hours a year of training. Math teacher McLaughlin said his professional learning has included leading professional development for colleagues on preparing students for the ACT exam. "I was surprised at how many teachers who had been working for 20 years didn't know benchmarks for their subject area," he said, "didn't know what their kids should be able to do in order to avoid remediated classes." The district has teachers "cycle" through leading learning, a practice that has two sides, according to McLaughlin.

"Most of our professional development is led by teachers in our own school system," McLaughlin said. "One pro is that we get to see people we work with take on a different role and share things that they're very knowledgeable about. I think that it's a good thing in that it gets them out of their comfort zone and we can see what strengths we have. One drawback is we don't get a lot of new ideas or people who can shake up the system when it needs to be shaken."

Dean says it's important to rely on internal staff to provide professional learning.

"We believe that the people in our district are some of the most talented educators in the world," she said. "We've identified those high-fliers, based on the data—that she is a world leader when it comes to teaching math, he is a world leader when it comes to improving those AP scores, she is a world leader as far as being able to be effective with low-level students, and he is a world leader when it comes to moving those middle students.

"We let the data identify who is effective," Dean continued, "and we've tried then to use them for professional development and modeling for the rest of us."

LEARNING TO USE DATA

The district retained retiring administrator Gail Rice to act as a systemwide part-time data coach to help dig into the data. Each school formed a data team, and administrators meet regularly with each principal and teacher representatives to review individual building data. At first, Rice said, she presented school data to the staff. As the school-based educators became more familiar with how to look at the information, they began to take over the analysis.

Now Dean gives teams questions to consider, and team members search out responses to the questions. Teachers must analyze test results and have plans to address student deficits. Teachers at each primary school consider their data together in grade-level learning teams, Rice said, to identify staff members with strengths teaching certain skills and then to share those lessons. Teams at some schools now are able to present their own data to central office administrators.

"By doing it that way, teachers now own the data rather than [analysis] being something that happens in the central office or in the principal's office," Moorhouse noted. He said that has also allowed teachers to look at disaggregated data and take responsibility for those results.

ADDRESSING THE NEEDS OF DIVERSE LEARNERS

The district has addressed the growing English-learning population by making sure that each school keeps a close watch on data indicating student progress. Homing in on achievement gaps and tracking individual student progress is an expectation, administrators said. Students who fall behind are identified quickly and provided with interventions based on diagnostic assessments.

Dean said the district at first tried to hire more dually certified teachers to support students learning English but soon realized it would not find enough staff to keep up with the growing demand. Instead, administrators focused on changing expectations and improving instructional strategies.

"We are rural," Dean said, "and there are some people in the community who were not particularly welcoming [of non-English speakers]. It's truly been a situation that called for us as leaders in this district to examine ourselves and have the courage to do what is morally right. And it's not morally right to be part of developing another generation of second-class citizens. . . . Schooling is not a do-over. What we do by these kids in a large part is going to determine the life that they live."

The district leased two classrooms from the local community college and turned them into an International Center, where students initially can spend a half day learning English before returning to their home schools for the remainder of the day. Administrators trained a cadre of 60 teachers and administrators in Sheltered Instruction Observation Protocol for teaching English learners and then had them work with teachers in each building to learn the strategies, encouraging teachers to use those strategies to more effectively reach all students, including those with special needs.

"It's about thinking about your lesson, and if you're teaching third grade math, do you also have a language objective?" Dean said. "It's about the gestures that you use in your classrooms, how animated you are, and about how you use technology."

USING TECHNOLOGY TO SUPPORT LEARNING

Working with new tools through technology is another area the district is emphasizing, both for students and staff. The district's website has curriculum maps available for each grade and subject area, providing teachers with guidance on pacing, rigorous questioning, and formative assessments. The website also has links to shared lessons, both audio and video, as well as additional resources for teachers to enhance their lessons.

Moorhouse, for example, has lessons for teachers posted on the Morristown West website, linking teachers to model instruction that they can view anytime. Rather than spending faculty professional learning time on requirements that don't focus on instruction, he places those lessons online for teachers as well.

"Things that have to be repeated every year like blood borne pathogens are set up on an Edmodo account," Moorhouse said. "Teachers will go in, view the video, take a quiz at the end, and we'll record that they passed the test on blood borne pathogens."

Moorhouse said the staff's use of technology has soared in the last decade, as grants have helped the system install interactive white boards in each high school classroom along with LCD projectors and document cameras. Ten years ago, he said, teachers' technology consisted of a shared phone in the main office. To help teachers integrate the new tools into instruction, the district has hired a dedicated technology coach.

USING INSTRUCTIONAL COACHES TO SUPPORT TEACHERS

The technology coach is one of five instructional coaches system-wide: One coach works districtwide with grades K and 1 teachers, another with grades 2 and 3 teachers, and another with grades 4 and 5 teachers. The upper elementary coach also is certified to teach English as a second language and so supports teachers in providing instruction that benefits English language learners. The fifth coach works with secondary teachers.

What is important about the instructional coaches, Dean said, is that they don't function as reading teachers or assistant principals. These coaches support teachers through modeling, co-teaching, and feedback.

Coaches meet with all new teachers to develop "plans of progress," supplementing the support new teachers receive from monthly meetings with their mentors. For teachers who receive low-level performance evaluations, the coaches offer the feedback of an external observer and support on specific areas in which the teacher needs improvement. Some coaches also offer voluntary sessions during teachers' lunchtime to provide training on specific strategies.

Coaches have focused on helping teachers districtwide increase the level of rigor in their lessons, including changing how student learning is assessed. They have presented research about improving formative and summative assessments, working with teaching teams at each grade level.

Based on feedback from the instructional coaches and from principals, the district also might decide that a grade-level or subject area's teachers need to come together for districtwide training. The district provides substitutes for half-days in order for teachers to gather for these trainings, sometimes several times a year. Other learning sessions take place over the summer.

The coaches themselves meet together with the director of professional development each Friday afternoon for two hours in their own learning community. They gather around a table with a whiteboard and markers to make notes on areas teachers are struggling with or to review data. They leave a running list up and determine what professional development should be offered based on their observations.

"We talk about our data; we talk about what we're going to learn next," Dean said. "We're reading the same thing, and that keeps us all on the same page and it keeps us on the same page as a district."

GAINING PERSPECTIVE THROUGH LEARNING LABS

Instructional coaches also use the district's two learning labs to teach lessons, inviting a class to the lab, videotaping the lesson, and then sharing the result with teachers throughout a school or across the district by posting it on the district website.

The labs are one of the more cutting-edge ideas in place in Hamblen County. In Manley Primary and Manley Intermediate schools, teachers have access to a classroom with a 360-degree camera affixed to the ceiling that allows them to videotape a lesson to a computer or iPad.

The two schools had open rooms that allowed them to be outfitted as labs. Part of the funding came from federal Department of Education Race to the Top money, but when those funds expired, Lynch said the district had to make a critical decision about whether to continue paying for the labs with local money. He said he made the determination based on his own experiences with athletes.

"I was an old ball coach," he said, "We spent a lot of time breaking down plays, watching tapes to try to get our kids to be better. I've taken that same mentality in a nonthreatening environment where teachers can watch their own teaching practices, watch the work of their students. I really think that this is a tremendous opportunity" for teachers to improve instruction.

Teachers in the two buildings are asked to tape and view a lesson each term. Teachers tape themselves and then can review the tape when they choose. They may choose to keep the lesson private or upload it, sharing it with others or with their principal as an element of their evaluation. Some of the videos, with the teacher's permission, are posted on the district's website as exemplary lessons for all in the district to see.

Other teachers also may access the labs. A Morristown West High School math teacher who teaches freshmen honors students, for example, recorded several lessons and provided them to middle school teachers to help them prepare students for the extra rigor of the high school curriculum. A kindergarten teacher at one school who had been researching reading techniques arranged to bus her class across town to the lab and tape a lesson that then was shared across the district.

The lab is especially helpful, Dean said, for teachers to analyze how different groups of students may respond to a teacher's instruction or whether the teacher may unconsciously face one side of the room more often than the other.

"I can see to whom do I ask questions? To whom do I ask follow-up questions?" she said. "Is there a difference in the level of questions that I ask to this group of students or to that group of students in my classroom? Sometimes when we watch ourselves or hear ourselves and hear how we pronounce words, it can make a difference in how we are with a group of second language students.

"It's pretty hard dealing with seeing it sometimes," she continued, "but I think it helps teachers to get better. It's one thing for you to tell me I didn't ask as many follow-up questions to girls in my classroom, and I never asked more than a Level One question to a special education or a second language student. It's another for me to see that for myself."

Lynch is slowly expanding the labs. A renovation at Morristown West High School will include cameras in every classroom in the new addition, and Lynch hopes teachers will avail themselves of the opportunity to watch their own lessons.

HIGHLIGHTS OF HAMBLEN COUNTY DEPARTMENT OF EDUCATION

- The district was awarded the 2012 State Collaborative on Reforming Education prize for most dramatically improved student achievement.
- Hamblen County was one of four Advanced Placement Honor districts in the state in 2011, recognized for increasing access to AP courses while maintaining or improving the rate at which students achieved a score of 3 or higher.
- Morristown East High School was named a National Blue Ribbon Award winner in 2005, Morristown West High School in 2011, and John Hay Elementary was honored in 2012.
- *U.S. News and World Report* recognized Morristown East with a Bronze Award (2007, 2008, and 2009) on its best high schools list; Morristown West received a Bronze Award in 2008 and Silver Awards in 2012, 2013, and 2014.
- Average ACT scores for the district in 2013 were 20.0, as compared with Tennessee's 19.5 and 20.9 nationally.
- Director of Schools Lynch was named one of "20 to Watch" in 2012 by the National School Boards Association's Technology Leadership Network.
- The Tennessee Organization of School Superintendents named Lynch the 2014 School Superintendent of the Year.

MAKING SURE EVERYONE IS A LEARNER

Lynch's tenure in the district has added to its stability and the possibility that projects such as the learning labs will continue to grow. His decade-plus at the helm has been combined with consistency on the school board. Six of the district's seven elected board members have remained the same throughout his tenure, with the seventh the child of a deceased former board member. Lynch stresses that board members are re-elected because voters feel secure in their leadership—that his is "not a status quo board."

Lynch said leadership in learning starts at the top—with the board. Board members continue their learning by attending state and national conferences and have annual retreats to examine district data. The result of their learning is usually a new way for the administration to look at its work.

The retreat "always generates a lot of questions and some additional research," Rice said, "because no matter how much data you give them, there are always five things they think of that they really want to see and that we haven't broken down in that particular way."

Lynch said board members fully understand the value of professional development.

"It starts in the board and goes all the way to the classroom," Lynch said. "When you don't have a board of education who understands the importance of professional development for themselves, for their superintendent, and for the teachers, it's not going to work. Because then when you go through tough budget times like all schools and communities do from time to time, sometimes those are the first areas that people look within the budget to cut.

"But to have highly effective teachers, you have to have that quality professional development," he continued. "You have to have that as an expectation. Through expectations, you will see results. I think that's what we're doing here."

THE VIEW FROM THREE SEATS

BRENDA DEAN, assistant director of schools

When I first came here, professional learning was, "Let's ask the farm bureau to do an agriculture demonstration that could be used in the classroom or the dairy council to do something about milk, and let's see who we can get to do it for free." We were always looking for somebody outside ourselves to provide a lesson that wasn't necessarily aligned with our curriculum needs—and it certainly wasn't data driven. We had a zero budget in professional development in those very lean years. Sometimes the state would provide training.

Around 2005, we began strengthening our professional development in relationship with Harvey Silver and Richard Strong, taking Robert Marzano's work and making it easily translatable to a classroom teacher. Since then, we've become huge consumers of educational literature and research. But reading about it isn't enough. There is an old expression that says sitting in a henhouse doesn't make you a chicken. We decided that the way we were doing professional development wasn't improving our instruction. It was like we were sitting in the proverbial henhouse.

What we needed was to move to job-embedded professional development, and with instructional coaches working with learning teams, we could provide on-time assistance to teachers. The idea is to solve problems as close to students as you can. Honestly, I think instructional coaches have been the most cost effective thing we've ever done. If you want professional development for your school around writing, you don't have to go to a third-party vendor; I'm going to send you Stephanie to provide that on-time professional development. Our staff have been to Columbia's Teachers College for training and elsewhere, and our coaches are highly skilled. We can offer quality professional development on an array of topics.

The other part of improvement is expectations. Our superintendent has really led us into a no excuses culture. We're never going to say that funding is the reason why we didn't do it, why we didn't achieve it. The fact that our demographic has changed, that we have more poverty, that we have more second-language students—none of that is going to be our excuse, *ever*.

BRADLEY BAYS, social studies department chair, Morristown West High School

The district has a lot of professional development during the summer, and our school has a day before school starts where we focus on what's being required, such as with the Common Core. What's helped change the mindset of teachers in the department, though, is not just the training that gets put on from the central office, it's what they've been willing to do for us outside of that.

When we were part of High Schools That Work, we actually got to go visit schools. Our administration has also been in quite a few schools to see what they were doing with Advanced Placement, with assessments. Visiting other schools showed us some things to improve on and what we were doing right. Other schools have been coming to see what we are doing, too.

We've been encouraged to visit teachers in our same subject areas and have dialogue. I've talked a lot with a member of the AP microeconomics

(Continued)

(Continued)

committee who teaches about an hour away. I meet with him two or three times a year, and in between, we have email contact. We'll say, "I'm having *this* problem in my class. What do you do?" In addition, the administration encouraged me to become a macroeconomics reader for AP exams. This allows me to spend a week not only with fellow AP macroeconomics and microeconomics teachers, but also with economics professors.

We also have gone to conferences, which helps because we were able to hear other schools present. We have instructional coaches that cover us for different areas. We have one for secondary who lets us know every week what is coming with the Common Core, what to pay attention to.

We don't have formal department meetings in social studies. Occasionally teachers have common planning, but most of the time [getting together] can be a before or after school thing, or we eat lunch together.

Really what we've done in our school the past couple of years is to work together to try to make learning more accessible to everyone. We admire that mindset of "Let's find reasons that people can actually do this. Let's not use poverty or any kind of category to stop us."

Our assistant principal didn't even tell teachers which students were predicted to score below basic or basic one year because we didn't want that expectation to weigh us down. That's why I like working in Hamblen County. It wasn't always this way, but now when people ask me what sets us apart, I say, "We're not in the excuse-making business. We really believe that it is possible" for all students to achieve.

DALE LYNCH, director of schools (superintendent)

I have been fortunate enough to serve on the Tennessee Organization of School Superintendents, which has allowed me to work with other districts across the state. Through work with other districts, I've grown personally and professionally. As a result, I have made sure that our principals know how important it is that they visit others schools in the district at least twice a year to work with other school leaders.

This past year we also had a system in place in which our principals visited one another's schools and co-evaluated staffs, and that was probably, according to our principals, what they felt was their biggest area of opportunity. I also highly encourage them to make it a part of their professional growth plan to go outside the district to see other schools. In addition, 90% if not 100% of our teachers will go outside of their building to observe better practices from other teachers across our district. We hire substitutes for that purpose. It's an investment that's not that expensive.

We need to seek these opportunities to look outside. We are not on an island. As educators, we need to make sure that we know and understand the importance of collaboration. As administrators, we have to make that point first with leaders and then we can do it with teachers.

In Hamblen County, we have built relationships across the state and country and have had the opportunity to see some really good practices from other districts. Every day I find out that I need to know a whole lot more than I did this past year. That's the biggest part of being adult learners—that we have to make sure that we continue to evolve and learn as educators in our school district.

Note: Quoted material from Bradley Bays, Brenda Dean, Dale Lynch, Brian McLaughlin, Jeffrey Moorhouse, and Gail Rice is used with permission.

CASE STUDY DISCUSSION QUESTIONS

1. What impact does the district's no-excuse mission, which ensures ALL students learn at high levels, have on educator's professional learning?

2. What learning designs did Hamblen County use? Which district designs intrigue you? In what ways could the district strengthen its professional learning experience?

3. How does Hamblen County determine which designs are effective in improving teacher practice and effectiveness? How will you determine which designs are effective?

4. What questions does your school or learning team need to ask to be able to select learning designs appropriate for your needs?

5. What learning designs does your school or learning team have in place now? In what ways could existing designs be strengthened?

6. What does job-embedded professional learning mean to you? Which of the district's designs would you consider job-embedded? Which current learning designs that you use would you consider job-embedded?

7. How does the school board in Hamblen County support professional learning? What difference does the school board's support of professional learning make within the district?

8. Hamblen County strongly supports visiting other schools and other districts. What are the benefits of these visits?

Index

CORWIN

A SAGE Company

The Corwin logo—a raven striding across an open book—represents the union of courage and learning. Corwin is committed to improving education for all learners by publishing books and other professional development resources for those serving the field of PreK–12 education. By providing practical, hands-on materials, Corwin continues to carry out the promise of its motto: **"Helping Educators Do Their Work Better."**

Advancing professional learning for student success

Learning Forward (formerly National Staff Development Council) is an international association of learning educators committed to one purpose in K–12 education: Every educator engages in effective professional learning every day so every student achieves.